PACKED for the WRONG TRIP

PACKED for the WRONG TRIP

A NEW LOOK INSIDE
ABU GHRAIB
AND THE CITIZEN-SOLDIERS WHO
REDEEMED AMERICA'S HONOR

W. ZACH GRIFFITH

Arcade Publishing • New York

Arcade Publishing books may be purchased in bulk at special discounts for sales promotion, corporate gifts, fund-raising, or educational purposes. Special editions can also be created to specifications. For details, contact the Special Sales Department, Arcade Publishing, 307 West 36th Street, 11th Floor, New York, NY 10018 or arcade@skyhorsepublishing.com.

Arcade Publishing® is a registered trademark of Skyhorse Publishing, Inc.®, a Delaware corporation.

Visit our website at www.arcadepub.com.

10 9 8 7 6 5 4 3 2 1

Library of Congress Cataloging-in-Publication Data

Names: Griffith, W. Zach.
Title: Packed for the wrong trip : a new look inside Abu Ghraib and the citizen-soldiers who redeemed America's honor / W. Zach Griffith.
Description: New York : Arcade Publishing, 2016.
Identifiers: LCCN 2015047251 (print) | LCCN 2016002330 (ebook) | ISBN 9781628726459 (hardcover : alkaline paper) | ISBN 9781628726466 (ebook)
Subjects: LCSH: Abu Ghraib Prison. | Iraq War, 2003-2011--Prisoners and prisons. | Maine. Army National Guard. Field Artillery Battalion, 152nd. | Soldiers--United States--Biography. | Prisoners of war--Iraq--Biography. | Soldiers--United States--Social conditions. | Prisoners of war--Iraq--Social conditions. | Iraq War, 2003-2011--Regimental histories--United States. | BISAC: HISTORY / Military / Iraq War (2003-). | HISTORY / Military / United States. | HISTORY / United States / 21st Century.
Classification: LCC DS79.767.D38 G74 2016 (print) | LCC DS79.767.D38 (ebook) | DDC 956.7044/37--dc23
LC record available at http://lccn.loc.gov/2015047251

Jacket design by Laura Klynstra
Front cover photograph © Getty Images

Printed in the United States of America

This book is dedicated to the men and women of the Armed Forces, current and former, whose physical, mental, and emotional sacrifices transcend the politics that send them into harm's way, and to the memory of those we've lost. *Semper Fidelis.*

CONTENTS

ONE

FIRE FOR EFFECT

"My fellow Americans, major combat operations in Iraq have ended. In the battle of Iraq, the United States and our allies have prevailed. And now our coalition is engaged in securing and reconstructing that country."
—President George W. Bush, May 1, 2003

ONE THOUSAND one . . .

Dizl saw the inside of a human head.

Another explosion ripped open the ground like a thunderbolt from a vengeful deity.

The head belonged to an Iraqi man who had recently—very recently—departed this earth and was now moving through the air between sky and sand. If death separates a human soul from the body, then this man's soul had certainly gone on to better things by the time Dizl turned and saw the body cartwheeling on the upward thrust of explosives-displaced air. The man's head, transected laterally, opened and closed like a Pez dispenser, and his brain slid out toward the dusty ground.

William "Kelly" Thorndike was a sometime clam digger, blueberry raker, offshore fisherman, hotelier, elementary school gym teacher, emergency services dispatcher, preschool teacher, prison guard, and longtime artist. But at that moment he was a US soldier affectionately called Dizl by his comrades, two of whom were weathering the storm of shrapnel with him.

Dizl was a Fort Benning soldier by trade: a ground-pounding infantryman, a grunt who'd found himself attached to an artillery battalion filling the role of untrained military police officers.

The other soldiers had taken to calling him "Private Major." The title was a mash-up of the lowest-enlisted rank (private) and the highest (sergeant major). When they stepped off to Iraq, he was one of the oldest men with the lowest ranks among those shuffling onto the plane. The allusion to the prestigious rank of sergeant major came from Dizl's ability to think above his rank, to take past experience and apply it to the clusterfuck that was their time at Abu Ghraib. He also had kids older than the eighteen- and nineteen-year-old privates he bunked with.

Dizl, middle-aged and a father of four, was a private in the 152nd Maine Army National Guard Field Artillery Battalion. Mobilized just before Christmas and sent to the Middle East, Dizl's unit had arrived in Iraq in February of 2004. Field artillery refers to those units in a modern army that use large-caliber guns (originally catapults, more recently cannons, missile launchers, and howitzers) for mobility, tactical proficiency, and long-range, short-range, and extremely long-range "target engagement." Basically, a FAB (field artillery battalion) exists to support the infantry from twenty miles out with things that go *boom*.

For various reasons Dizl and his unit been sent to war with orders completely different than the unit's original training and purpose. The 152nd FAB had been sent to a detention facility in Iraq that none of them had ever heard of, where they would serve as military policemen (MPs).

Dizl's unit was trained to drop ordnance on enemies from a distance. On what should have been the bright side, "detainee operations," unlike field artillery, is supposed to be an MOS (the acronym for "military occupational specialty," their way of making "job description" sound more impressive to prospective recruits) that does not expose one to battlefield conditions. Detainee facilities are not supposed to be sited anywhere near areas of active combat—one reason women are permitted to serve as MPs. But during the year of their deployment, the American detention facility at Abu Ghraib would come under fire from mortars, rockets, snipers, and suicide bombers virtually every day.

They would also be subjected to two assaults that resulted in what the military calls mass casualty events; so many people, soldiers, and detainees were injured that medical personnel had to triage survivors—find those who had a chance at survival, and separate them from those on the losing end of a mortal wound.

When the first of these mas-cas attacks began, Dizl was on duty with fellow soldiers Turtle and Sugar. The three men were up in the Hawk's Nest, Tower G-7-1, which overlooked the portion of Abu Ghraib prison known as Camp Ganci.

Predominant among Ganci's detainees were thousands of Iraqis picked up by Army and Marine units during missions throughout Iraq in the fall and winter of 2003 and 2004 and dropped off at Abu Ghraib. Many were undoubtedly Bad Guys—die-hard Saddam loyalists, native religious fanatics, or specimens of the Syrian, Yemeni, or Saudi jihadists who had come over the unsecured borders of Iraq after the invasion.

According to later US military intelligence, however, most (estimates ranged between 60 and 90 percent depending on the political leanings of those making said estimates) of the detainees shoehorned into Ganci were noncombatants with little or no intelligence value. Thus, statistically speaking, it is probable the man who flew and died in front of Dizl's eyes was an ordinary citizen who, whatever his personal feelings about the end of Saddam's regime and the presence of American troops on his home soil, had merely been caught in the wrong place at the wrong time. It had cost him his life.

Picked up and plunked down at Abu Ghraib, where no reliable mechanism yet existed for sorting the relatively innocent from the definitely guilty, he and his fellow detainees had shared their tents and dismal days with strangers, supervised by Americans who had recently acquired a worldwide reputation for brutality, torture, and sexual abuse. As if all this weren't enough, the detainees were sitting ducks for insurgent attacks, targeted with no evidence that the attackers wished to spare their lives.

On this particular morning—April 6, 2004—the insurgents were firing 120 mm mortars into the middle of Ganci from a position beyond the multi-lane highway that ran along the southern perimeter of the facility. The attack itself lasted perhaps thirty minutes, but time doesn't fly when mortars do.

One thousand two . . .

Dizl saw the man's brain falling, and he glimpsed the underside of the empty brain cavity. Then the body landed head down, like a lawn dart. The force of the explosion had dislodged the man's legs from their sockets at the hip and they were flapping freely before falling to rest on either side of the remains of the torso and forming a disfigured tripod of human flesh and bone.

Dizl took his eyes off the body in time to see another mortar explode and shouted at Turtle and Sugar, "Hit the deck!" He crouched over them, using his body to shield theirs from the chaos.

The mortars were "walking" toward the tower with the heedless, unstoppable power of a striding giant in a nightmarish fairytale. Between explosions Dizl raised his head and peered over the edge of the tower wall and watched the impacts burn orange in the center as high explosives threw rocks, air, and shrapnel outward through flesh and bone faster than the speed of sound.

One thousand three . . .

Turtle and Sugar, their views restricted by Dizl's body, demanded details.

"What's going on?" Sugar shouted from beneath Dizl.

It was what the military calls "fire for effect." After a round landed and exploded, spotters on the rooftops in the town of Abu Ghraib would use their cell phones to report the results and offer suggestions for targeting adjustments to the mortar team, who would be set up well downrange and out of sight. Rules of engagement (ROE) prevented soldiers from taking out these spotters, a skill each could have performed without scratching through the surface of their abilities.

Krump

Krump

Captain Morgan's tower, down near Ganci 2-4, was bracketed by a pair of explosions.

"What's going on?"

"Morgan is . . . Ganci 2 just got smoked."

One thousand four . . .

Two mortars landed in the center of a detainee tent about 150 meters from the tower—*Krump*—and a gaping hole opened up in the ceiling of the tent as smoke billowed out of both entrances and shrapnel tore ragged holes through fabric and flesh alike.

"What is . . . ?"

Krump

The hajjis are flying . . .

It wasn't just the man with the opened skull; the air was full of people and parts of people, along with metal, stones, and dirt. A five-ton army truck and the detainee water tower in the center of Ganci took direct hits. Rocks and shrapnel chewed up the thirty yards between the impact and Dizl, striking the tower's walls with a loud *whap* while the truck burned, belching greasy black smoke into the sky.

The mortars were carving a destructive path through Ganci in twenty-five- or thirty-meter intervals. Fire for effect. The cell phone spotters would be calling it in: "Give it another thirty meters . . ."

Krump

". . . another thirty . . ."

Krump

"On target. *Allahu akbar!*"

The Hawk's Nest was next in line.

Dizl saw the inside of the man's skull. He heard the rocks knocking at the tower door. He crouched over the two younger soldiers, the older GI carrying on the timeless tradition of the grizzled warrior protecting the young guys. Reflexively, he closed his eyes tightly and gritted his teeth. Gazing up into his face, interpreting his expression, Turtle and Sugar understood; the giant was walking closer. They were screwed.

TWO

THE WAY LIFE SHOULD BE

S ADDAM HUSSEIN WAS a vicious man who had ruled Iraq with enthusiastic brutality (together with an oil-funded selective largesse) since attaining the office of president in 1979. He made extensive use of Abu Ghraib during his reign, finding it a convenient location in which to confine opponents and dissenters (including Hussein Shahristani, a nuclear scientist who refused to help Saddam develop the WMDs that weren't there),[1] a place where his thugs (and sometimes his sons) might torture and execute their countrymen and still be back in Baghdad in time for supper.

---

1 Peter Galbraith, *The End of Iraq* (New York: Simon & Schuster, 2007), 142.

Having been at odds with the United States for a decade, he greeted the September 11 attacks with satisfaction, describing the day to one of Iraq's state-controlled newspapers as "God's punishment." But it bears repeating that Saddam was not an Islamic extremist. He wasn't even much of a Muslim except when political expedience demanded a show of piety. (Osama bin Laden loathed him and was offended when the Kuwaitis accepted American help in 1991 rather than give the job of expelling the Iraqis to al-Qaeda.)

When Paul Wolfowitz, architect and advocate for George W. Bush's Iraq policy, likened Saddam to Hitler, Saddam was doubtless flattered. The twentieth century's dictators Hitler and Stalin were his heroes, but whatever fantasies he may have indulged in, Saddam remained a Hitler wannabe and a mostly local threat. The rationale "We have to fight them in Iraq so we don't have to fight them in America" gave Saddam far too much credit. In fairness, we might also mention that Saddam's regime initiated social reforms that led to drastic decreases in the nation's rate of illiteracy and genuine improvements in the status of women.

Still, as would so often be noted by those pressing for the invasion, Saddam tortured and murdered thousands of his citizens, used chemical weapons against the Iraqi Kurds, and deliberately trained his two favorite sons to torture the family's enemies, apparently introducing them to sexual torture as soon as they were out of puberty.

Saddam's family of origin was what an American might call a dysfunctional blended family. Saddam's stepfather was reputed to be a real asshole, though whether he made a more regrettable male role model than Saddam's birth father would have done will never be known: Bio-Dad was out of the picture before Saddam was born.

Suffice it to say that cruelty was already an entrenched Hussein family value by the time Saddam himself, at the age of twenty-seven, was held and—he would claim—tortured in an Iraqi prison. Once he gained power, Saddam would be judged excessive even by his peers in a region known for the harshness of its regimes.

"The enemy of my enemy is my friend," may be an Arab saying, but it has been a universal principle of diplomacy. The United States supported Saddam in the fight he had picked with the Iranians during the 1980s, but then, nobody seemed to like Iran. They had a scary ayatollah for their leader and had held Americans hostage. The then Soviet Union, China, and especially France all backed Iraq too, and Donald Rumsfeld wasn't the only foreign official who would later have to explain away his grip 'n' grin photo with the Butcher of Baghdad.

Eight years and hundreds of thousands of casualties later, the Iran–Iraq war ended in a stalemate, with Saddam in debt up to his eyeballs. Hoping to forcibly squeeze revenue out of some oil-rich territory along the disputed border with Kuwait, he floated the notion of invading that country to American ambassador April Glasspie. Glasspie gave a tactful but discouraging answer that Saddam, unluckily, mistook for a green light.

When the United States came to Kuwait's defense and attacked Iraq the first time around, the first President Bush really did have a broad, international Coalition of the Willing—willing, that is, to actually fight alongside our troops. Of the fragile coalition dragged into the sandbox by Bush II, only the British were genuinely able and willing to shed blood for the cause.

Sadism is not a traditional American value. Torture has been explicitly repudiated by the American military establishment dating all the way back to General George Washington's admonition to his hard-pressed troops to treat even the most villainous British prisoners of war with generosity and respect. Moreover, Iraqis in general were not meant to be our "enemies." Rather, they were named the primary beneficiaries of the invasion, a people whose oppression and longed-for liberation became our eleventh-hour *casus belli* once

Saddam's connection to al-Qaeda and his stockpiles of WMDs had both been proven nonexistent.

For symbolic reasons alone, Abu Ghraib's notoriety among Iraqis might have been taken into account when choosing a place to confine persons suspected of rejecting our gift of freedom. "We had extraordinary concerns about using a facility with this kind of reputation," admitted Brigadier General Janis Karpinski, the later-to-be-disgraced commander of detainee operations in Iraq, but apparently these concerns weren't extraordinary enough.

Faced with a sudden, urgent need to house and interrogate a surprisingly large number of suspected intransigent "back-sliders" (the administration had not yet admitted that they might be called "insurgents"), the US-led coalition decided to make use of facilities already in existence rather than go to the trouble and expense of new construction. So to this, the haunted House of Ravens and Strange Fathers, America imported our own ghosts and demons.

If Charles Graner could claim to have been motivated to enlist by the terrorist attacks of 9/11, so could Dizl and many other Americans.

At the same time, it was 9/11 that inspired the re-definition of "prisoner of war" and "torture" by Bush administration lawyers, and it was 9/11 that justified the Bush Doctrine of preemptive war. The president repeatedly referred to 9/11 in ways that forged a mental link between the hijackers who had killed and injured thousands of Americans and the dictator who was injuring and killing primarily his own citizens on Iraqi soil. By the time of the invasion, 63 percent of Americans believed that Saddam Hussein was responsible for 9/11.

Civilian employees of the Coalition Provisional Authority in the Green Zone in Baghdad consumed their high-calorie and strangely pork-heavy, Halliburton-supplied, American-style meals beneath a wall mural depicting the Twin Towers framed within the outstretched wings of a bald eagle. It was the publication of a sermon praising the 9/11 attacks that provoked L. Paul Bremer to close the offices of the Mahdi Army's newspaper *al Hawza*, which led to a stunningly bloody uprising of the Shia in Baghdad. And, as Dizl would note without pleasure, the disgusting and dangerous detainee compound known as Ganci had been named after New York City fire chief Peter Ganci, who died with his men in the World Trade Center on 9/11—a dubious honor for a good man.

To emphasize the presence of love in war is not to deny the horror, injustice, and suffering of warfare, nor the cruelty and carnage that are its character. Rather, it is to point out that even the most horrific, depraved, and wasteful of human behaviors do not and cannot eliminate love. Love simply exists within these environs, as it exists everywhere. And yes, sexual love is included, but it appears in other, far more significant forms too. Love offers safety, food, shelter, conversation; it is also the disturber of conscience, the seat of judgment, the impetus toward mercy, and the yearning for redemption.

Unbeknownst to anyone, *redemption* (and not merely damage control) would prove to be the mission of the 152nd at Abu Ghraib. Evil happens, as it happened at Abu Ghraib, in real time with real people inflicting and experiencing real pain. If we would claim that the 152nd succeeded in its mission—claim that redemption, honor, and, yes, love was not just possible but *present* at Abu Ghraib—it must be demonstrable, a spirit made manifest in the material reality of the human beings that breathed, drank, ate, walked, spoke, slept, dwelled, and died there.

The men and women who belong to the National Guard are by and large the same men and women who serve their communities in other ways. While sometimes looked down upon by insecure active-duty service members, National Guard and reservist units have a distinct advantage that active-duty units do not. While a majority of the active military is young and inexperienced outside of their time in the military, reservists come from various occupations outside the military. Police officers, firefighters, prison guards, construction workers, and all sorts of other skilled professionals can bring a myriad of experiences to the battlefield with them when called up from their civilian lives. The 152nd had a dynamic group of men that brought a variety of skills to the table. These Mainers could use their skills from home to fill the numerous gaps left by a lack of support from "Big Army."

"Our guys had a wide variety of abilities," said Mike Lord, the 152nd's serious, bespectacled first sergeant (known for obscure reasons as Huladog). "We had everything from a satellite engineer to computer programmers, plumbers, and electricians." It comes partly from a Maine culture, he explained. "There is a tradition of self-reliance, a tradition of being able to adapt, overcome, and repair just about anything with duct tape and string."

One of those men serving alongside Dizl was a young man named Shawn Keyte. He got out of high school and served for three years in the Army as an active-duty soldier from 1991 to 1994. He spent a year as a civilian before enlisting with the Maine National Guard in 1995. One weekend a month, he donned his uniform and trained with his Guard unit, unknowingly preparing not for the common civil relief missions, but for war.

Shawn worked for the Dexter Shoe Company in (surprise) Dexter, Maine. At the same time he worked for the shoe company, he also trained and worked as a firefighter and EMT for the Dexter Fire and Ambulance Service. These skills would, incidentally, prove useful a decade later in Iraq.

In 2000 Shawn landed a job with Frito-Lay in Bangor. He would drive a delivery truck on a route through western Maine. Shawn drove along country roads through woods and farmland, past little rivers and old mill towns and the hamlet of Monson. Here, Kim and Mike, the owners of Spring Creek Barbeque, would offer Shawn a pulled pork sandwich. He was so skinny, Kim was sure he would starve to death before he got to Greenville.

Coming up over the rise just by the Greenville trading post, the dramatic panorama of Moosehead Lake would fling itself out before his windshield in summer blues and greens, or immaculate, glimmering winter white. It was a satisfying sight.

Shawn was a happily married man with a baby daughter when the events of September 11, 2001, shocked contemporary America the way December 7, 1941, and the Japanese attack on Pearl Harbor shocked our parents and grandparents.

The national discourse became more combative, and when the White House started banging the modern war drum—with press releases and breaking news conferences—Shawn assumed and accepted that his country would soon be expanding the terms of his service. He was right. His country would send him to Abu Ghraib.

Andy Hazen started a microbrewery in the barn attached to the old Maine farmhouse he shared with his wife and three children in the '90s. Fortunately located in the high hills above Penobscot Bay, where views extend all the way to Cadillac Mountain and Little Deer Isle, it was (and remains) a family-owned and -operated business.

By the turn of the millennium, Andy's son Ben had graduated from high school, done three years of active service with the 82nd Airborne, and was helping his father brew four different ales and a nice porter between college classes in forestry and weekends spent training with the Maine Army National Guard and the volunteer fire department. When Ben was sent to Abu Ghraib, therefore, he was missed, not only because his family loved him, but because the business couldn't really spare him. In addition to Andy Hazen's natural worry for his son's safety was the added irritation of having his son deployed to fight in a war that Andy considered a bad idea.

When Huladog was ten years old, his father went off to serve in Vietnam. As a young man, Hula had enlisted in the Marine Corps, and he carried that esprit de corps through his entire military career. *Once a Marine, always a Marine,* after all. Whatever reservations he might have had about military service were trumped by the news that Iraq, under Saddam Hussein, had invaded Kuwait.

When his enlistment was up, Huladog became an intelligence analyst for, among others, the Drug Enforcement Administration. He possessed the useful skill of being able to take disparate bits of information—the jottings in a drug dealer's notebook, for example—and recognize the patterns that yield information.

After Hula left the Corps, he signed up with the Maine National Guard, which, like the rest of his men, put him on track to one of the most infamous places in modern memory.

Turtle had been a public school teacher in civilian life, instructing eighth graders in English and gym before his country decided it needed him at Abu Ghraib. He wrote letters to his college sweetheart, Alicia, whenever he had the chance, and when he wasn't writing to her—his short legs braced on the sandbags stacked against the walls of the Mortar Café, a spiral-bound notebook balanced on his knee—he was generally talking about her.

War is terribly boring, and one cannot keep an eye out for mujahideen and read, so men and women in the armed forces use conversation to pass the time. The best topics usually involve the usual disgusting things that adolescent males—and members of your military—enjoy. And girls; soldiers love to talk about their girls. Every warrior, stretching back from Iraq II to the first dust-up between tribes of our nomadic ancestors, has talked—at length—about their girlfriends (long-term or single evening).

So Dizl and Sugar would eventually know all about Turtle's plump, sable-eyed paragon. They'd learn her middle name, her high school accomplishments (all-state band, soccer team captain), her college GPA, her plans for the future (law school), and her opinion of the war in Iraq (not good). Indeed, Alicia would eventually take on mythic dimensions, occasionally appearing in their dreams, cast as an angel and, depending on the dreamer, bringing either the intimate or maternal care they longed for.

"Say hi for me," Dizl had said to Turtle, minutes before the first mortar fell that fateful April day, and Turtle had added a note into the sweat-smeared margin.

The literary standard to which Turtle aspired was high. He was a Civil War buff, Joshua Lawrence Chamberlain of the 40th Maine was his hero, and the letters written home from Antietam, Richmond, Gettysburg, and Appomattox to nineteenth-century farm and fishing families in Maine were his models. That he could claim ancestors who fought for the Union, as well as a grandfather who served in the Second World War and a father who, like Huladog's dad, fought in Vietnam, needn't surprise us. Soldiering, like medicine, firefighting, and politics, tends to run in families.

The effort of composing prose that both met this high standard and conveyed his affection to his true love made Turtle's rather high forehead pucker and his small, shy chin retract farther into the moist, salty folds of skin that tended to stack themselves between his jaw and the upper edge of his body armor. The visual effect was of a turtle pulled partway into its shell, which explains his nickname.

If Dizl, at forty, was the oldest member of the 152nd, Richard Parker was one of the youngest. The last of four children, Parker joined the Guard and was deployed virtually as soon as his high school graduation ended. Tall, lanky, with a thousand-watt smile, he was already a chain-smoker—not uncommon in the military. But this didn't seem to affect his physical fitness scores; he could run like a deer, which the more aged soldiers attributed to his youth rather than to his actual skill.

Like many boys growing up in the predominantly rural and small-town environment of central Maine, Parker liked the outdoors. He enjoyed hunting and fishing in the expansive Maine forests. When he was old enough, he discovered the invigorating, adrenaline-spiked joys of riding a snowmobile across the wide, white expanse of a snow-covered Maine lake. He collected fossils and stamps. But what Parker really liked to do was read. He brought fantasy books about dragons and elves with him to Iraq. It was here that Dizl introduced him to the strangely appropriate desert fictions of Frank Herbert's Dune series.

Dizl enjoys doing nice things for people and does so without any expectation of repayment. It was and remains one of his most steadfast traits; it is not uncommon to find him organizing art therapy for fellow veterans or helping his neighbors improve their gardens. He's a big, friendly, blue-eyed man who regards and moves through the world with the humble self-confidence of one who knows how to do a lot of useful things well. He does, conversely, walk with a limp.

The limp is from an injury to his ankle sustained at Abu Ghraib, and he has a scar on his chest where he got hit with shrapnel. However, Dizl's most severe war wounds are invisible. Like thousands of other American soldiers who served in Iraq, Dizl sustained what is known as a traumatic, closed-head brain injury, or TBI. He sustained the injury when a mortar shell exploded too close to him. He was outside the lethal zone of the shrapnel, but the concussive force of explosions can be just as damaging. The wave of air pressure passed through him and physically bashed his soft brain against the hard bone walls of his skull. It is one of the most common injuries our service members are returning home with.

A TBI is by definition neurological damage. Post-traumatic stress disorder is also the result of neurological damage. Except in Dizl's case, the PTSD was caused not by concussive force but by the toxic neurochemistry of prolonged stress; the stress of imminent death, the concern he had for his fellow soldiers, and the strain of being responsible for thousands of inmates in the middle of a war changed the way Dizl's brain would work forever.

Mental illness and neurological disorders are the unseen casualties of war. In the worst cases, leaders ostracized soldiers who came forward looking for help for their mental injuries. Contrary to popular belief, PTSD is not an inevitable pathology of the combat vet, but it is a fairly common one. Dizl's got it. It hurts. However, Dizl sometimes says that PTSD was the price he paid for his brain keeping him alive. It's the mark of a combat vet, and he holds some pride in the ailment.

Dizl has what is sometimes known as a photographic memory. It has been both a blessing and a curse for him. It is useful for remembering policies and procedures from more than two decades of holding various jobs (including prison guard) and being the standard "Maine Man," taking on a variety of useful tasks like gardening and carpentry. But it is a curse, because there are things that he'd like to forget, but his brain won't stop the movie reel in front of his mind's eye.

To complicate the matter, he now also suffers from severe short-term memory loss. He can remember what time he woke up and what he had for breakfast in 1983. But he can't remember conversations that happened in the last forty-eight hours.

These men made up the 152nd—the uniquely Maine-ish group that would be responsible for turning a controversial heap of humans' rights abuse and murder into a fully functioning and (relatively) humane prison.

Previous visitors to Maine who have found themselves unable to stay away will cross the Piscataqua Bridge from New Hampshire these days and be surprised by a new message appended to the old Welcome to Maine sign. It now reads: OPEN FOR BUSINESS.

This is not the welcoming sign most Mainers know, remember, and miss, and it certainly was not the heart-stirring motto that the

152nd Forward Maine National Guard Field Artillery Battalion carried with them to Abu Ghraib.

Despite its pockets of deep poverty, Maine remains a place where people live because it is beautiful, and because it retains its own distinctive version of a traditional New England spirit, one that balances independence and interdependence, individualism and community responsibility. The old welcome sign summed up the state and the pride it prompts in its citizens:

MAINE—THE WAY LIFE SHOULD BE

There are three broad categories of armed persons that the US Army can bring into play when our civilian government tells it to go to war: active duty, the National Guard, and the reserves. The Navy, Air Force, and Marine Corps have similar force structures, though the Marine Corps doesn't have a National Guard component. A basic distinction can be drawn between those groups who perform federal missions exclusively (the regular Army and the reserves) and the National Guard, which exists first to defend and assist the citizens of a given unit's home state.

Though the National Guard falls under the operational support of the reserves, it is the state's governor who has the authority to call up the Maine National Guard when, for example, there is catastrophic flooding in Aroostook County. The National Guard undertakes federal missions—war in Iraq or Afghanistan, for example—only at the specific behest of the President of the United States.

National Guard troops were supplementing the active military in overseas engagements long before September 11, notably in the Balkans in the late 1980s. Still, during the war in Vietnam, service in the Army or Air National Guard was a way to avoid overseas deployment rather than a way to guarantee it.

Indeed, because of the reserve and National Guard's historic role as supplement and backup rather than front-line, the bureaucracy at Big Army did not place the highest priority on equipping and training them. The shortages of body armor and equipment that so famously plagued the full-time military in Iraq would be even more problematic for the reserves. Reservists got the leftovers or hand-me-downs. Some of the gear issued to members of the 152nd came stained with blood.

The Maine Army National Guard's 152nd Forward Field Artillery Battalion wasn't originally destined for Abu Ghraib. They weren't even supposed to go to Iraq. By the time the 152nd was called into service, the President of the United States had publicly declared Iraq to be a country in which combat operations had been successfully concluded. By definition, a field artillery battalion is a combat unit. Thus, in keeping with its structure and purpose, the 152nd was destined for Afghanistan where, as of the end of 2003, there was still unquestionably a war on, if an increasingly neglected one.

Activated in the winter of 2003, the Mainers had begun training at Fort Dix for battle against the Taliban and al-Qaeda in the slush and snow of a New Jersey winter. "It was a bit of a head-scratcher," Huladog said. "There was always snow and the temperature was below zero."

Pretend what's underfoot are rocks and sand, not snow! Pretend you've got body armor and radios to communicate with, pretend these soda cans are 155 mm howitzer shells. Pretend that training in hand-to-hand fighting with broomsticks is an adequate substitute for training with real weapons. Pretend there is heat in your jeep. Any questions? OK, good, BOOM—you guys over there are dead.

In addition, the training they were receiving at Fort Dix had little to do with their mission once they went forward. There, they were given lessons in first aid, protection from chemical and biological and nuclear weapons, land navigation, and convoy protection.

They were trained and tested on the firing and maintenance of a variety of weapons, including the M16 assault rifle, the M9 Beretta handgun, the M249 light machine gun, the M203 grenade launcher—most often seen as an under-the-barrel attachment of a rifle—the MK-19 grenade launcher, and the "maw-duce" M2 .50 caliber machine gun.

Of course it was important for them to practice driving in formation, route reconnaissance, reacting to ambushes, and all the other skills one would like to have in the proverbial toolbox before stepping off to war. They were, after all, going to be working in a theater of operations where they would be under attack from un-uniformed insurgent groups via their favorite weapon: the improvised explosive device.

"In an insurgency, it is the political result that is always paramount. Though devastating physically, the most significant effect of roadside bombs was that they made US troops wary of operating among the people. The fact that insurgents were able to place so many bombs, often repeatedly along the same stretches of road, also made a political statement, because it meant the locals weren't reporting on them. Coalition forces are forced to interact with the Iraqi populace from a defensive posture, effectively driving a psychological wedge between the people and their protectors," Major General Peter Chiarelli, who commanded the First Cavalry Division in Iraq in 2004, observed.[2]

However, not only were most of their classes given via hours of PowerPoint lectures (a mind-numbing experience known as "death by PowerPoint"), some of the education they were receiving was incorrect. It turned out they spent hours learning phrases in the wrong dialects for the region they would be deploying to. Many of them wouldn't find this out until they tried out their new linguistic skills on uncomprehending detainees.

---

2 Tom Ricks, *Fiasco* (New York: Penguin, 2007), 221.

A week before the scheduled deployment to Afghanistan, word came down. The Maine reservists would be going to Iraq instead, to a place none of them had ever heard of.

"Abu . . . what?"

"Abu Ghraib. It's a detention facility. A prison."

"What do they need a field artillery unit for?"

"Nothing."

"What are we going to do?"

"We'll tell you when you get there."

When informed, at last, of the destination and duty awaiting his men, Captain Phillip Trevino also made one of what were to be many behind-the-scenes attempts to acquire some extra hands-on training and experience with prison equipment for them. Once he realized they were about to be transformed into military policemen doing detainee ops, Trevino wangled a field trip to the local federal penitentiary.

Except for Dizl, few of the members of the 152nd had ever set foot inside a correctional facility of any kind, and Trevino figured that the tour might offer at least a glimpse of what the care and control of prisoners actually looked like. Trevino also managed to arrange for a training session from civilian corrections officers in a skill that goes by the ominous name of "extractions." This is what is required when a recalcitrant inmate refuses to come out of his cell upon request.

New Jersey's felons did their best to resemble captured terrorists, snarling, eyeballing, and assuring the touring soldiers that horrible wounds and death awaited them in Iraq even as stateside wives and girlfriends were seduced away.

"How long you gonna be over there? A year? Dang, man!" said one.

"How long are you going to be in here?" Turtle responded.

After taking a moment to mull this over, the prisoner decided his feelings were hurt and muttered, "Don't have to get personal about it."

The captain's abhorrence of the "check-in-a-box" style of training became well known among the training command staff at Fort Dix. While Hula said that the instructors had all the sincerity and desire to teach their deploying comrades the skills required to survive in a war zone, they did not have the required support from higher command.

At one point, Hula was informed by a series of irate sergeants major and colonels that if he didn't get his commanding officer in line, Captain Trevino would be relieved of duty. The military loves checked boxes. Whether they indicate actual acquisition of knowledge or not boils down to the small-unit leaders ensuring actual education. Captain Trevino and Hula were hell-bent on making sure their soldiers had the tools they needed to survive.

Big Army—feeling the heat from the secretary of defense's office—had other ideas and was keen on getting the 152nd forward in the most expedited manner possible, and the pressure could be felt all the way down through the ranks. Like his or her civilian counterparts, a military police officer is normally put through an application and screening process intended to weed out druggies, weirdoes, and people with criminal histories. The ones who make the cut are sent to a military police academy, running a prison.

But all of this takes time and time was one of the resources squandered in the run-up to the war. Suddenly in need of many more MPs than the military had available, field artillerymen were made into prison guards on the strength of whatever bits of training could be stuffed into them before and during their deployment.

Military training in a new skill follows a formula: familiarization, practical application, and then a demonstrated execution of new skills. For example, airborne units will practice jumping out of planes using platforms a safe distance above the ground before even stepping into an airplane. The movements and techniques are drilled into soldiers so that they become second nature, requiring no thought as they step out of a perfectly good airplane for the first time. Even then, people have been known to go splat.

By this standard the men of the 152nd were not just poorly trained, they were untrained. They were not briefed on the layout of Abu Ghraib, nor the character and distribution of its population, nor on the security situation that awaited them. Much, however, was made of the Geneva Convention and the necessity of refraining from photographing detainees. Three days of hastily concentrated classes passed in a forgettable blur. Certificates were distributed with disproportionate fanfare, allowing public-affairs officers to tell the press, straight-faced, that only "certified" prison guards were working in Iraq.

Captain Trevino received a flight time just over five hours before departure; he still had men out in the field undergoing their pre-deployment training.

"You men squared away and ready to go to war?" an enthusiastic colonel asked Hula.

"No, sir," the first sergeant said to the much higher-ranking officer, "I still have men in the field."

Quietly but firmly, Captain Trevino also made a small protest when he refused to sign the certificates before the unit stepped onto the tarmac and headed off to war without that final check in the box.

This lack of training was an eerily common theme among deploying units, not just the 152nd.

Discussing the Jessica Lynch debacle, "The unit was not trained to be in the situation they were in, was not equipped to be there, no GPS [global positioning system, a satellite-guided navigation system], no radios, no training on crew-served weapons, only one crew-served weapon in there, no night vision gear," was the harsh but accurate judgment later delivered by General Peter Shoomaker after he became the Army Chief of Staff. [3]

"We didn't know how to go to war," Hula said. "The last major war they'd had was Vietnam and it'd been so long that many of our generals came from administrative jobs. They didn't even know how to prepare their men."

They had no after-action report meeting, no way to adjust the training for the better for the next units to rotate their way though on their way to Iraq. The high-ranking officers in charge wanted to hear nothing that could be improved; they wanted men pushed through to theater.

When the plane had lifted off and begun arching toward Camp Virginia, Kuwait, the entire contingent of soldiers cheered. "Why are you all so excited to go to war?" asked a pretty stewardess for the chartered aircraft bringing them across thousands of miles of ocean and strange lands.

"We're not," Hula explained to her. "We're just happy to be leaving Fort Dix."

That cheer, Hula said, summed up about the entire Fort Dix experience.

---

3 Ricks, *Fiasco*, p. 119.

THREE

THE 'GHRAIB

"All told, more than three thousand suspected terrorists have been arrested in many countries. And many others have met a different fate. They are no longer a problem for the United States and our friends and allies."

—President George W. Bush, January 2003

FIRST SERGEANT MIKE Lord, a.k.a. Huladog, was responsible for the overall well-being of the soldiers under his command and offered his men the following advice as a prophylactic against losing one's mind in preparation for their time in Iraq: "The smart soldier lives by the three-hour rule," he'd say. "Three hours from now, you'll probably be doing something different than what you planned."

It might be a tiny change, Huladog explained, a mere tweak to the standard operating procedure (SOP), or it could be a completely and massively revised mission. Either way, it's a FRAGO, short for "fragmentation order." It's the Army way.

There is an idea that many of the soldiers we send into harm's way are poor people whose desperation recruiters are wont to take advantage of, or that men and women fill the ranks whom judges have given the choice "go to jail, or enlist."

While military service has been shown to help an individual move up the economic ladder, in fact enlisting for an all-volunteer military has higher demands than many people think. Sadly, the minimum requirements of having a diploma and a healthy body can be hard to meet for kids growing up in places that offer little access to education and health care. Criminal history and drug use are more common in poor communities and are added hurdles to a military career. Admittedly, though no public-affairs officer will confirm or deny, such standards tend to slacken a bit when the economy is robust and offers more alternatives, or when America has overextended itself as, for example, by fighting wars in Afghanistan and Iraq simultaneously.

That being said, members of our armed forces nonetheless tend to come from the middle and lower-middle classes. Contrary to popular belief, minorities comprise a smaller percentage of the military population than of the general population. Perhaps less surprisingly, so do women. Certainly there are financial motivations for military service, but the Army, Navy, Air Force, and Marine Corps, as well as the Coast Guard, offer additional attractions for young men and women, not the least of which is the chance to participate in one of the few remaining institutions in American life in which words like "service," "honor," and "courage" are used without irony; most join for selfless reasons.

The United States invaded Iraq in March 2003 alongside President Bush's now somewhat infamous coalition of the willing. While US forces technically had forty-eight allied countries backing them, the only countries other than the United States to put boots on the ground were the United Kingdom, Australia, and Poland. Our other allies would eventually send ground units once the initial invasion was complete.

By May, President Bush considered the results of the invasion and the removal of Saddam Hussein from the seat of power sufficiently successful enough to allow him to make a public declaration that the war was over. He became the first standing US president to make an arrested landing (using a metal wire stretched across the landing deck of an aircraft carrier, which catches a hook on the tail of the plane to slow it down and prevent it falling off the other end of the runway upon landing). He arrived aboard the USS *Abraham Lincoln*, an aircraft carrier anchored off the coast of California, in a Lockheed S-3 Viking—a craft used by the US Navy to identify and track enemy submarines.

It was aboard the *Abraham Lincoln* that Bush delivered his victory speech. Behind him, forming a backdrop for the phalanx of television cameras, was a large banner reading MISSION ACCOMPLISHED.

No matter how loud and proud that banner may have been, in 2004 the wars stretched the US Armed Forces thin and generals were pulling National Guard units to serve active-duty roles in jobs they hadn't trained for. This is not uncommon in any of the services, where individual service members are often pulled from their desk or infantry jobs to serve as prisoner escorts, security, personal drivers, bus drivers, cooks, and all other manner of duties. "Adapt and overcome" is the unofficial motto of the military.

Objections to the deployments of National Guard soldiers and active-duty service members on their third and fourth combat tours were met from the pro-war side with an argument along the lines of, "Well, you joined up because you wanted the money, and now you're complaining that you might actually have to fulfill your commitments." Those whose complaints were overheard by soldiers of superior rank would often have the addendum "sack up."

In the same month that Bush declared the war won, the 372nd Military Police Company, based in Virginia, was deployed to Iraq. Among these MPs were Specialist Charles Graner and Private

Lynndie England. The 372nd would spend the summer training new Iraqi police officers at Al Hillah.

Al Hillah is an ancient city described as the location of the tomb of the prophet Ezekiel. But it is also the site of a mass grave containing the bodies of thousands of Iraqis who had been murdered a dozen years before the arrival of US troops by Saddam Hussein's security forces.

However, as the summer came to an end, the 372nd was subsumed into the 800th MP Brigade. Under the command of (Reserve) Brigadier General Janis Karpinski, this unit was given the new responsibility of providing care and control of prisoners at the Baghdad Correctional Center.

Recently commandeered by the Americans, the prison was known colloquially as Abu Ghraib, a garbage-strewn complex of grayish-brown buildings clustered within 280 acres of gray-brown, gravelly sand and surrounded by a twenty-five-foot-high grayish-brown concrete perimeter wall. Atop the sand lay a few inches of gray dust that the wind would whip into a gritty fog and rain would turn into mud the sticky consistency of pizza dough. The whole world of Abu Ghraib was gray.

In Arabic, Abu Ghraib most often means "Place of the Raven," though it is sometimes also translated to "House of Strange Fathers." Either would seem an appropriately sinister appellation for what amounted to Saddam Hussein's Lubyanka, but in fact the name did not properly belong to the prison itself.

Like the old Maine State Prison in Thomaston where Dizl had worked, the Baghdad Correctional Center was known by the name of the nearest town, though Abu Ghraib is a big city by Maine standards, boasting 180,000 residents, and located about twenty miles northwest of Baghdad.

The name Abu Ghraib was briefly mentioned in the American press during the first Gulf War, when a factory in the city was suspected of producing not infant formula but chemical weapons agents. The same factory, having been rebuilt, was proffered when the Bush administration was presenting its evidence that Iraq possessed weapons of mass destruction in the run-up to Operation Iraqi Freedom. (As of this writing, no evidence of anything but baby milk has ever been discovered there.)

British contractors, creating a facility that offered convenient proximity to the capital so that Saddam's secret police could make frequent and ruthless use of its amenities, built the prison in 1960s.

By the time of the American invasion, these "amenities" included torture and gas chambers. There was also a breezeway used as a shooting gallery and a room outfitted with a two-scaffold gallows for quick, efficient, simultaneous hangings.

Adjoining the hanging room was a cluster of cells in which condemned men would await execution. These rooms were far too small to permit an adult to recline, so prisoners would sit and wait, watching other convicts die in pairs while awaiting their own execution.

Not surprisingly, given its nightmarish past as one of Saddam's go-to sites for torture and murder, Abu Ghraib was energetically looted during the generalized disorder that followed the fall of Baghdad. The looting and violence prompted the hurried resurrection of Abu Ghraib as a place to hold rioters and malefactors. Saying "Abu Ghraib" in Iraq can manifest the same feelings that saying "Auschwitz" can bring to survivors of Hitler's holocaust; at least one hundred thousand prisoners of Saddam's state were liquidated there according to Army Public Affairs.

The torture and execution chambers would be turned to other, more benign purposes once the Americans took over (Dizl would eventually sleep in one, for example), but the building known as the Hard Site was kept in service. The Americans began to use its three tiers of barred cells to house "high value" captives thought to possess actionable intelligence about a rapidly growing insurgency. The

Hard Site was also the place where problem prisoners from the general prison population could be temporarily sequestered.

Throughout the autumn of 2003, mystified by the increasing strength of an unforeseen insurgency, officials from the White House began to exert tremendous pressure on soldiers in the field to capture sources of HUMINT, or "human intelligence." Obligingly, soldiers and Marines scooped up any and all likely candidates and dropped them off at Abu Ghraib. This wound up packing the facility with more detainees than its understaffed, underequipped, and untrained personnel could safely manage.

Marines would be on patrol and an RPG would go ripping by overhead, so the Marines would go in the direction of the point of launch. They would sometimes find a soccer game or other community gathering and ask, "Who the hell shot that at us?" Of course, no one would answer so the Marines would go, "OK motherfuckers, all of you are coming with us now," and the people would end up in Abu Ghraib. Next thing allied forces knew, there were eighteen thousand prisoners stuffed into a space the size of the Samoset Resort.

In addition to the intense pressure from Washington came a "wink-wink, nudge-nudge" that gave intelligence units throughout the theater of war the idea they had free range to use more intense methods of detention and interrogation that had been condemned and even prosecuted as war crimes under previous American administrations. The prison became the filter through which the entire war on terror was designed. The language in the rules of war changed to incorporate the new "rules." Rumsfeld changed the language of "POW" to "detainee" so the United States could legally keep prisoners of war in a war zone.

The resulting damage to human lives and to America's strategic interests and moral authority in the world remained deniable until the damage was exposed, up close and personal, at Abu Ghraib.

On November 7, 2003, seven Iraqi men with bound hands and hooded heads arrived at Tier 1-A of the Hard Site; they were incapacitated, disoriented, blind, and terrified.

What happened to them that night would eventually be revealed to the whole world, and would be presented as irrefutable evidence that the United States had lost both wits and morals in the fearful aftermath of the terror attacks of 9/11 and was subjecting suspected terrorists to vile, degrading torture as a matter of routine.

In addition to the torture, a big problem with the Abu Ghraib scandal was that the seven prisoners were not, in fact, suspected terrorists. Rather, they had been yanked from a crowd of detainees rioting over the quality of food after a seriously mentally ill detainee identified them as the instigators.

These men were actually accused of ordinary crimes such as car theft and burglary. Understandably, these seven were doubtless getting fed up with awaiting trial by the new and improved Iraqi criminal justice system, and it is entirely possible that they really did start the food riot.

Since they weren't even suspected insurgents, however, these seven had no intelligence value to the American military. No military intelligence officer or contract interrogator would have had any reason to wish to interview them.

So the American soldiers present on Tier 1-A that night—Charles Graner, Ivan Frederick, Jeremy Sivits, Javal Davis, Sabrina Harman, Megan Ambuhl, and Lynndie England—had no rational reason to think they should "soften 'em up" for the purposes of interrogation. What's more, Sabrina Harman had the detainees' "face sheets" in her hand, documents that offered their names, detaining units, locations of detention, and the reasons these men were being held; it meant that the soldiers knew they were tormenting people who had no intelligence value.

One of the detainees, Nori Amir Gunbar al-Yasseri, had been jailed for rape, and Harmon was sufficiently cognizant of the fact to write the word "rapeist [*sic*]" on his buttock and thigh with a Sharpie. The MPs could not claim to have mistaken their subjects for anything but common criminals (at least officially).

Granted, an insurgent force is, by definition, not a uniformed fighting force, so there was no way for the soldiers to know for sure that these men were or were not enemy combatants. Such sentiment had been—and continues to be—the ad hoc excuse for service members who get carried away in their duties overseas. However, on paper, these men the soldiers were about to torture had no connections with the insurrectionaries.

The Iraqis were stripped, punched, stomped, placed in a variety of strange and humiliating positions, and forced to mime fellatio and to fondle themselves. The forced masturbation was a pornographic "gift" from Charles Graner to his girlfriend, Lynndie England, who would turn twenty-one when the prison clock struck midnight.

The soldiers deliberately and gleefully photographed their actions that evening, adding to the other similarly disturbing and now-familiar photographs taken at around the same time. Photos of the detainee cowering at the end of Lynndie England's leash, the hooded man standing on a box with wires leading out from under his clothing, and another menaced by an MP's snarling dog, would all become iconic images by early spring.

The pictures appeared on innumerable websites, posters, banners, and jihadist recruiting materials, inciting demonstrations and violence throughout the Muslim world. To this day, mentioning the words Abu Ghraib to most Americans—and, indeed, to many non-Americans—will likely elicit images of the now iconic photographs. Skinny, scared human beings curled and huddling, their fear written clearly across dirty faces, cowering from America's smiling heroes.

The name Abu Ghraib swiftly entered the English lexicon, sharing with My Lai and Kent State a similar history of members of our armed forces—men and women our country holds in high esteem—becoming not forces for good but forces for evil. It is, perhaps, this abrupt turn of the back to the service member's code of honor that makes incidents such as this so disheartening.

Maine National Guard chaplain Andy Gibson, a veteran of conflicts in Bosnia and Kosovo, and the father of an Iraq War veteran, prefaces his comments about the Abu Ghraib scandal with a long denunciation of the perpetrators of the abuse. "They were dishonorable, disgusting, undisciplined, culpable, and I'm glad they went to prison," he says. Then he pauses, to make sure this will be held firmly in mind during his ensuing remarks.

"But what Lynndie England and Charles Graner and the rest of them did was *nothing like* My Lai. It wasn't Babi Yar. It was not an atrocity. I've seen atrocities. I've been there when we opened Bosnian graves filled with the murdered bodies of women, children, and old men. The guys of the 152nd were picking up the bones of people Saddam murdered—*that* was an atrocity. What happened at Abu Ghraib after the Americans took it over was bad—but it wasn't even *close* to that."

Occasionally you will hear the Bad Apples of Abu Ghraib defended, if weakly, by people saying, "It was nothing compared to what they would do to us." This is true, if beside the point. Once Saddam Hussein was out of the action, and the weapons of mass destruction proved first elusive and then illusive, the rationale for the continued American occupation was that Americans are better, nobler, more honest and humane than them, no matter which "them" you have in mind—Saddam and the Ba'athists, al-Zarqawi and Al-Qaeda in Iraq, Muqtada al-Sadr and his Sadrists.

Baghdad had fallen. America and the Coalition Partners had the pick of the real estate. Maybe there were good intentions but bad judgment when it came to using Abu Ghraib at the beginning of the occupation: The place already existed and had the requisite features (cells and walls) already in place. It was centrally located and relatively close to the capital on land that Alexander the Great, Cleopatra, and a lot of other great civilizations coveted. In an area known as the Fertile Crecent, the Abu Ghraib prison estate sat squat in the middle of the birthplace of civilization.

However, Dizl and others wondered, how many mortar rounds had to fall before some bright soul remembered that the first duty of anyone holding prisoners of war "*is to remove them to a place of reasonable safety*" as section 1, article 20 of the Geneva Convention states?

"The problem of the Iraqi prisoners isn't only what is written in the news," a prisoner declared to General Miller and the press in May of 2004. In the absence of those photographs, how long would it have taken the American and international press corps to notice that the Iraqis we imprisoned, including children, were being blown up? If Abu Ghraib was convenient enough to Baghdad that tired Triton Corporation interrogators could retreat to the air-conditioned Green Zone between sessions with the Worst of the Worst, it could not have been too difficult for reporters to find it. So where were they? Only when the photographs surfaced did Seymour Hersh bother to look into the place, and once the photos had been revealed, no one was interested in anything else.

One of the questions that forced its way into Dizl's consciousness during the deployment continues to torment him to this day: *Was I part of the problem, or part of the solution?*

It is not an easy question.

His government had packed for the wrong trip, equipped him for failure and made him responsible for care he could not provide and control he could not properly exert. William Kelly Thorndike, a forty-year-old father of four, soccer coach, corrections officer, preschool teacher, and artist was forcing human beings at gunpoint to remain behind barbed wire in a filthy and demonstrably unsafe environment, and caring about them was going to break his heart. If he didn't die at Abu Ghraib then he was going to have to live with it for the rest of his life.

When Colonel Quantock was interviewed on NPR's *Face the Nation* in September 2004, he was asked to name the problems he found at Abu Ghraib. His list was a tidy summation of the horror stories Dizl and the Lost Boys of the 152nd can tell.

"The facilities were . . ." Quantock paused, perhaps sorting through some memory of one of the public-affairs office's media relations classes, and came up with "inadequate."

So when the *Lewiston Sun-Journal*, a Maine newspaper, reported the upcoming deployment of the 152nd, the article began, "There are 120 members of the Maine National Guard working at the Abu Ghraib prison in Iraq, but the Maine unit was not part of the alleged abuses there, a spokesman said."

The spokesman for the 152nd also said, "Our soldiers got there in mid-to-late February, which was after the scandal." He was also quoted as saying that the commander in charge of the Maine troops was "amazed" at the "heinous" acts of some of the soldiers who had preceded the Mainers, and reaffirmed "none of his soldiers were involved in any of that." Four of the seven sentences appearing in that short piece had the abuse scandal and the innocence of the Mainers as their explicit subject.

Between August of 2003 and February of 2004, the detainee population had quadrupled, and it was still increasing. The vast majority of the new detainees were now suspects in various violent "crimes against the coalition." They were young and old, followers and masterminds, Shiites and Sunnis, garden-variety mental patients and mad terrorists. As many as ten thousand men and perhaps about two dozen women were being held at Abu Ghraib, most of them—roughly seven thousand—confined in the portion of the prison known as Camp Ganci.

Ganci was a football field–sized rectangle of dull gray sand set into one corner of the prison. Bounded on two sides by the prison's twenty-five-foot wall, it was separated from the rest of the facility by a high, steel chain-link fence punctuated with manned security posts placed intermittently around the perimeter.

This area was further subdivided into eight compounds, arranged in two rows of four, each separated from its neighbors by unpaved alleys wide enough for two Humvees to travel down them side by side.

Each compound was overlooked by three observation towers and a command post and surrounded by three long, long rolls of concertina wire, stacked pyramid-style. Ingress and egress was possible through a steel access cage known as a Shark Cage (because these resembled the equipment used by Jacques Cousteau). Escapes had happened, so these barriers, however forbidding they might have appeared, could not be presumed impregnable.

There were water tanks set atop scaffolding and fitted with showerheads that served as "shower points" for the detainees' supervised bathing, and porta-potties for toileting. Shelter from sun and rain was provided by a number of white tents, which gave the area a spurious resemblance to old photographs of Civil War–era POW camps.

Major General Geoffrey D. Miller, who assumed command of all detainee and interrogation operations in Iraq in 2004, and Colonel David E. Quantock, who was given charge of detainee facilities specifically during the same period, had specific orders to clean house at Abu Ghraib in every possible way. Thus, during the year the Mainers spent in Iraq, many changes would be made that would take concrete form in a newer, more modern detainee camp. The new camp was promised to be, and in truth was, a huge improvement over Ganci.

Originally called "Camp Bison," General Miller would later decide to officially christen it Camp Redemption.

Ironically, the word "redemption" has no precise translation in Arabic. The closest match is the word *yandam*, which roughly translates to "let's not do this again." Nor does the theological concept of redemption hold much resonance in Islam, the majority religion in a country of thirty-five million.

Still, for a nation that arguably began losing its grasp on the democratic future of Iraq, it was appropriate. The name Redemption served as tacit acknowledgment of the now famous crimes committed by American "Bad Apples" at Abu Ghraib. If "Abu Ghraib" had become synonymous with American shame, "Redemption" captured the earnest American hope that disasters can be transcended, wrongs made right or at least better . . . and better late than never.

It would be up to the 152nd to take a place of infamous horrors and be the redemption the American government promised the Iraqi—and its own—people. Dizl and his men would carry the burden of loving their enemies on their shoulders. Because, in fact, it was their job to care for, feed, and protect the very men the United States had deemed evil.

Retired colonel Robert Rheault, former commander of Special Forces in Vietnam, explained the paradox that is the warrior's experience of war by saying, "There is a terrible contradiction in the experience. On the one hand, you and your finest, closest, most trusted and, yes, loved comrades, and you yourself, are functioning at the very top of your ability and effort, alertness, concentration, endurance, and courage—all this good stuff in the context of a situation where other human beings are trying to kill you, and you are trying to kill them."

Love offers safety, food, shelter, conversation; it is also the disturber of conscience, the seat of judgment, the impetus toward mercy, and the yearning for redemption.

FOUR

PACKED FOR THE WRONG TRIP

"The flow of equipment and personnel was not coordinated. . . . The unit could neither train at its stateside mobilization site without its equipment, nor upon arrival overseas, as two or three weeks could go by before joining with its equipment."

—Former secretary of defense James Schlesinger

TWO OBVIOUS AND enormously significant questions will be asked by any individual sent into harm's way in time of war, whether or not they are asked aloud.

Am I going to have to kill people?

Will I die?

Everyone dies, of course, but statistically most of us will die of heart disease or car accidents. Very few people die in explosions, blown to pieces that fly through the air, or by gunfire.

In films or on television, deaths produced by gunfire are remarkably athletic. Mel Gibson gets blown through a window or gunshot victims go flying through the air as Stallone stands alone against an army of bad guys, mowing them down with an M60 he holds in one hand. Reality is generally less ballistic. Whether hero or villain, if you are shot dead you'll fall down. Your face will express bewilderment, if it expresses anything at all.

A bullet is shaped to move through both air and flesh, and its mass will be insufficient, relative to the mass of your body, to pick you up and fling you through any handy plate glass windows. Bullets are small and devastating, but they are not nearly as theatrical as the action sequences of summer blockbusters.

On the other hand, when a mortar round or bomb goes up, the concussive force will send a heavy wave of air that is often powerful enough to throw people and vehicles around. The punch in a mortar, or the average Iraqi IED, is sufficient to shove a nearby, unshielded body irresistibly through anything that yields, or will simply tear it to bits. Still, the body, dead, falls down—in one place or in many.

Danger slows time, or at least the perception of its passing. Mortar attacks, like other traumatic events, are perceived in slow motion, second by second—one thousand one, one thousand two, one thousand three.

Am I going to have to kill someone? Am I going to die?

Of course not, the soldiers of the 152nd reassured one another, as they waited for orders to begin the trip to Abu Ghraib. In the first place, detainee facilities, what used to be called POW camps, are usually not situated near contested areas. In fact, the first duty of an army that takes prisoners is to remove said prisoners from the battlefield for their own protection. Thus, by definition, a detainee facility is the safest possible place to serve within the theater of war, even if that war is active and continuing.

"I can't tell you if the use of force in Iraq today would last five days, or five weeks, or five months, but it certainly isn't going to last any longer than that," the secretary of defense had confidently asserted before the invasion began.

A reduction in the overall level of violence in Iraq, noticeable during the midwinter of 2003–04, and linked in the minds of American commanders to the capture of Saddam Hussein in mid-December, seemed to confirm that the war—finally more or less acknowledged as a war, at least by the brass in theater—really would wind down and be over soon.

That same winter, a major rotation of American troops took place, and virtually all the units that had been in Iraq for a year departed. They were replaced by fewer, though fresher, troops.[4]

The month of February 2004, the very month that the 152nd arrived, boasted the lowest death toll of any month of the war thus far. However, this may have been due in part to the troop rotation that sent the 800th MP Battalion home and saw the Sixteenth MP Battalion—which included the Maine tradesmen, students, personnel managers, shop foremen, state employees, and health-care workers who made up the Maine Army National Guard 152nd Forward Field Artillery Battalion—rotated in.

Their stateside training deemed complete, the 152nd flew from the United States to Camp Virginia in Kuwait, landing in two planeloads, or "chalks," and disembarking onto sand that was blond, fine, and endless. The flight had gone without incident save for an overly enthusiastic young private who managed to slice his hand open while playing with a massive KA-BAR knife.

Upon landing, the soldiers were loaded up onto buses driven by local nationals who took to racing each other in the rickety vehicles stuffed with American troops. At one point Hula's driver managed to get to the front of the convoy of buses but didn't know how to get to their final destination and ended up lost in the desert and stuck in a sand dune.

---

4 Ricks, *Fiasco*, 321.

While Lieutenant Murray got himself spun up stressing over a defensive perimeter, Hula set about organizing a working party to push the bus out of the dune.

"First Sergeant," the lieutenant said severely though a quivering voice, "shouldn't we set up a perimeter and call for an evac?"

"With what, sir?" Hula asked. They had a bus full of trained soldiers, but only two of them were armed with a small handful of bullets.

They made it out of the dune and desert with no incident, and safely to their staging point where they would play the old military game of "hurry up and wait."

Nothing remained for the 152nd but gathering up their gear and crossing the frontier. Unfortunately, their gear was missing. Stacks and stacks of American conex boxes formed a huge, strange cityscape in the desert outside Kuwait City like the final scene of *Raiders of the Lost Ark*. Lieutenant Murray, Dizl, Turtle, and Skeletor spent most of a long, hot day wandering up and down endless rows looking for the conex box containing their equipment.

"It had a blue sticker and a red square," the lieutenant said, in what he hoped was an encouraging tone, when they determined for the thousandth time their box was not in the predetermined and agreed upon location.

"Blue sticker, red square," Turtle repeated, but the ability to recognize their own among thousands of virtually identical boxes waned as night drew near.

Before leaving, Hula had been reassured that the boxes had tracking devices on them should they be routed in the wrong direction. However, these only had a battery life that lasted a few days, so the signal unsurprisingly blinked out just days into its voyage from the United States to the Middle East.

The actions and failures of politicians in power have consequences: It is an idea we accept in principle. After all, it's why we vote. But the average civilian has only a vague awareness of such consequences. Numbers and statistics broadcast to the American people weren't vague political conjectures; they were real-life problems for men and women on the front line.

One of these problems was that a bunch of rapidly dehydrating Mainers wasted a day staggering around the sandbox outside Kuwait, seeking what Turtle insisted on calling their "lost luggage," which was still floating somewhere in the middle of the Atlantic.

Years of experience provides generals with what becomes common knowledge: If you're going to send Platoon X to the Middle East on an airplane, you have to make sure that an airplane of the appropriate size is ready to take off when the platoon arrives at the airport (with a contingency plan for mechanical failures or other glitches), and when the plane lands, there will have to be something for the members of that platoon to eat, wear, shoot, and poop in.

There are so many moving parts to account for: How many battalions, brigades, platoons, and units are available, and which will be activated and when? Where and by whom will they be trained, when will they be deployed to Iraq and by what means of transportation?

It is a monumental task organizing and transporting such massive quantities of Meals Ready to Eat (MREs), bottled water, water purifiers, rifles, grenade launchers, tents, trailers, helicopters, tanks, trucks, spare parts, hammers, nails, porta-potties, bullets, helmets, body armor, socks, bottles of insect repellent, toilet paper, medical kits, maps, gasoline, soap, ballpoint pens, night vision goggles, anti-malaria medications, batteries, extension cords, sunscreen, and more.

Every item has to be either sourced in-country or purchased. It has to be inventoried, packed, accounted and signed for, loaded into cargo vessels, and shipped across the ocean where it must be unloaded and matched specifically with units as they arrive. If this gets screwed up, you can have a lot of guys without gear and gear without guys.

To be sure, planning a war is incredibly complicated and it only gets worse when, for instance, the Office of the Secretary of Defense insists on overruling plans that have been months in the making.

It is common knowledge among troops in the field that when politicians untrained in the ways of war get involved, things have the potential to (at best) become a bigger headache, and at worst cost the lives of their brothers-in-arms. The men who send boys off to war often have no concept of the potentially lethal consequences of ignoring such ancient advice as "Plan according to the fight, fight according to the plan."

Of course, finding the conex box wouldn't have made much difference to the Mainers since, as Dizl explained, they packed for the wrong trip anyhow. Their box mostly contained equipment suited to the original mission for which they had been trained and prepared: kicking in doors in Kabul. Abu Ghraib presented a new and unexpected challenge, one which would call for another bit of ancient military wisdom: Adapt, improvise, and overcome.

They had no communications gear, very little medical gear, some chemical warfare boots, and a "dandy" set of weapons racks. They also took possession of old-fashioned flak jackets, which they planned to use to reinforce the doors of the soft-sided trucks that would be their transportation to Abu Ghraib to provide a modicum of protection from shrapnel and small-arms fire.

Eventually, they would be issued Kevlar vests supplemented by two ceramic plates, one for the back and one for the chest. Some of the vests arrived with only a single plate, however, so the soldier wearing it was forced to ponder whether he was more likely to face fire from in front or behind.

They did have a large supply of ammunition, which raised another question among some of the men: how smart would it be to load all this explosive ordnance into a bunch of trucks with canvas doors and convoy them down a highway known as "IED Alley"?

Lieutenant Murray, who would later receive the unfortunate nickname "Lunch Lady" owing to his agreeable habit of bringing food with him when checking on his soldiers standing duty at Abu Ghraib, decided it wouldn't be quite smart enough.

"Let's find a place to leave it instead," he said. "This is stuff that needs to be transported in secure vehicles. I'll find a depot we can leave it with."

They had three Humvees assigned to them for the task. The ammunition had been loaded, but they had not yet received the keys to unlock the steering columns to drive them. The liaison kept promising that we would get the keys day after day with no results.

Lunch Lady got fed up waiting; the time had come to move their ammo. "Technically we were stealing the trucks," he recalled, "but the mission required it so we cut the locks." Lunch Lady didn't expect any reprimand for the "theft"; besides, he planned to be out of the area long before anyone found out.

Now informed of an appropriate spot to store their ordnance and hijacked vehicles, Lunch Lady and a few intrepid Mainers set off for a military depot somewhere on the far side of Kuwait City. Within minutes, they had become hopelessly entangled in the spaghetti of freeways woven amid the urban sprawl. Everywhere they looked were people who, from a perspective warped by months of training and the dehumanization of the enemy, looked an awful lot like terrorists.

Back at Fort Dix, they had been given laminated pocket cards printed with various useful phrases to use when communicating with Middle Eastern civilians, and Skeletor and Turtle had conscientiously studied these. Maybe if they were ambushed and kidnapped they could converse their way out of trouble?

Night fell. They were still lost. At one point, Turtle looked through the windscreen at the monster high-tension wires choking the sky and channeling power all the way to Europe. Turtle announced that if they were attacked by jihadists hell-bent on stealing their truckload of ammo, he planned to fire a grenade at the nearest electrical tower.

"I bet it would turn all the lights out in France," he said. "That would get some attention."

It was a cheering thought. They pressed on.

Had they been forced to stop and ask directions, the Kuwaitis would probably have been as kind and helpful as possible. Some might even have spoken English, as Kuwait is a wealthy country and part of a world community in which English is the common coin. Besides, however exotic men in kaffiyehs and women in headscarves might have looked to the Mainers, military trucks full of uniformed Americans were old news to Kuwaitis.

As it turns out, it was probably a fortunate thing that Lunch Lady at last figured out how to find the US ammunitions depot without stopping to ask. Unbeknownst to Dizl and the other soldiers, the army had issued the wrong language cards. The phrases Turtle and Skeletor had so carefully memorized ("Who dwells in this house?" "Please place your hands above your head." "Thank you.") were in Farsi. Farsi is the language of Iran, Iraq's oldest enemy.

"Packed for the wrong trip," as Dizl would say.

Nothing exciting happened while the small group was gone, except for an incident involving Private King, whom the lieutenant had left behind on gear security. "I suppose he did pretty well for the day," Lunch Lady said. "Other than the fact that I noticed that he convinced himself it was OK to use my electric shaver. I was in shock. His reasoning was that he had never used one and that he didn't think I would mind. He was counseled [a euphemism for a disciplinary ass-chewing], but luckily he was moved from my platoon shortly after."

It is common practice for commanders near the end of their unit's deployment cycle to cut back on the riskier endeavors they'd been sending their troops out on up to that point; casualties do not look good on FitReps—fitness reports that determine whether or not a promotion or commendation is waiting upon their return. Neither troops packing for departure nor those unpacking on arrival are likely to be out on patrol, engaging the enemy in firefights or making forays into hostile territory along roadways mined with IEDs. So the reduction in the number of casualties, however welcome, promoted a sense of progress that would prove illusory.

The Iraqis who'd challenged the American occupation in the summer and fall of 2003 and survived gained valuable and lethal combat experience. The Americans were thinking the fight was over; the insurgents were gearing up for round two, taking their defeats of the previous months and turning them into learning opportunities.

Even given the relative quiet, commanders decided it was too dangerous to send the whole of the 152nd up IED Alley by unarmored trucks. So the majority of the men would travel from Kuwait to Baghdad by plane, with a small group left behind to convoy the equipment a few days later.

As they prepared to board the transport that would fly them from Kuwait to the Baghdad International Airport, known as BIAP (pronounced Buy-Yap), the Mainers met some guys on their trip home. One was limping along on a shattered foot, his shaved head engraved with an enormous, livid scar.

"How was it?" the newcomers asked.

The man shook his head, his eyes giving a textbook demonstration of the "thousand-yard stare" they had heard so much about.

"It's not what you think," he said. "It's not what they've been saying. It's a shit storm."

FIVE

WELCOME TO THE MORTAR CAFÉ

"Following their arrest [by Coalition Forces], the nine men were made to kneel, face and hands against the ground, as if in prayer position. The soldiers stamped on the back of the necks of those raising their head. They confiscated money without issuing a receipt."

—International Red Cross report, February 2004

ABU GHRAIB WAS hot, filthy, smelly, overcrowded, ugly, infested with vermin, teeming with bacteria and viruses, strewn with garbage and raw sewage, lacking in basic medical facilities, and prone to dust storms, mud baths, drought, and flooding.

It was hot; the average daytime temperature was 133 degrees Fahrenheit, which was miserable for a group of people used to the mild, pleasant Maine summer where temperatures exceeding 80 degrees were a rarity to be endured rather than the norm. Like any other combat deployment, it was dreary and boring. The initial excitement of arrival quickly receded and breaks from the monotony came in the form of anything that was even remotely out of the normal.

The 152nd would be serving with four other companies: the 301st MP Company from Puerto Rico, the 428th MP Company from Indiana, Marine Corps K CO, Third Battalion Twenty-Fourth Marines from Missouri, and 391 Headquarters Company from Columbus, Ohio. Each unit would be assigned various duties in Abu Ghraib. The Marines guarded and patrolled the main perimeter, the MPs would control and guard the detainees, and Headquarters Company took care of logistical operations such as mail, food, and supplies.

As if all the heat, disease, and garbage didn't make life there hellish enough, Abu Ghraib would be the focus of some of the most frequent and intense insurgent attacks in the entire Iraq theater. Despite the Marines guarding the perimeter and patrolling the town of Abu Ghraib, everyone at the prison complex was vulnerable to mortar rounds, VBIEDs (car bombs), and snipers. To make matters worse, their gear was not only inappropriate for their mission, the 152nd was completely missing equipment vital to the safety of both the soldiers and their prisoners.

Among the tools the newly minted MPs from Maine lacked were radios. They had a few sets of old hand-crank radios that relied on wires for transmission, which were vulnerable to sabotage. Astonishing as it seems, the spotters surrounding the complex could be calling in the firing coordinates by cell phone, probably texting their wives at the same time, but there was no way for soldiers working in Ganci to communicate with any other soldier beyond the range of his voice.

Turtle's dad, back in Maine, heard about this. Restraining any impulse he might have had to drive to Washington, DC, and personally ream out Donald Rumsfeld, he drove instead to LL Bean in Freeport, where he purchased four crayon-colored Motorola walkie-talkies (the kind marketed to parents who want to keep track of their kids on the ski slope) and mailed them to Iraq.

These had disadvantages. The relative importance of communication, observation, and self-defense had to be continuously and literally juggled given that the radio took one hand to operate. They also weren't as sturdy as they might have been. After Dizl got blasted during the major insurgent assault of April 20, his radio never worked properly again. Nor did the binoculars Dizl's brother had sent him. Or his right eye. Still, the Motorolas were a whole lot better than nothing at all.

FRAGO: You know those malaria pills we gave you three weeks ago and required you to take every day? They'll make you sick. Stop taking them.

On his first morning at Forward Operating Base, Abu Ghraib (FOBAG), Dizl went for a walk around camp. He'd slept fitfully the night before. Which was no surprise given that his platoon had been told to live in a building known as the Mortar Café. Originally it had served as the cafeteria for Saddam's prison, then as the dining facility for the American contingent originally charged with refurbishing the vandalized property for use in detainee operations. Halliburton subsidiary Kellogg Brown & Root (now KBR, Inc.) had established a new and presumably more modern kitchen and dining facility, so the Mortar Café was free for use as living quarters.

When the remnants of the 800th MPs had finished clearing out, Dizl's platoon (First Platoon) would move into their quarters, known as an LSA (short for "living facility"), and set about trying to make it feel a little like a home away from home.

So Dizl slept the first night behind concrete walls tastefully decorated with a large mural of Saddam on the outside of the building and the legendary "Welcome to the Mortar Café" scrawled on the inside. Their quarters were filled with a number of permanently installed concrete picnic tables, so there was no need—or space—for setting up cots.

It was a bluebird day, unusually clear and relatively cool by Iraq's standards, and Dizl was inclined to be optimistic as he wandered out across the helo pad, noticing the sparrows, the spiders, the crows. He gazed with interest at the rows of wire fencing surrounding and enclosing the detainee compounds, and at the makeshift soccer pitches and the tall tower of the mosque in the nearby village.

The detainees' tents looked a little like downscale circus tents, he thought, or maybe like the tents caterers provide for the reception after an outdoor wedding, if you subtracted the dirt, the trash, and the stench of raw sewage. The detainees seemed calm enough, although he had to admit, the range of ages was disconcerting. A very old man hobbled by, supported by an awfully young boy.

Is this a prison, or a refugee camp?

Chain-link fences and piles of glittering razor wire lined his path once he left the trash-strewn area in front of their new sleeping quarters. Some of the guard towers looked almost like children's forts cobbled together from material scavenged from a scrap yard.

He spotted Lunch Lady coming along the lanes between the enclosures, finishing up his own little walking tour. *We can compare notes back at the Mortar Café*, Dizl thought, and gave Lunch Lady a wave.

He spent a little time gazing meditatively at the open area known as Mortar Field, which someone had told him once served as a mass grave during Saddam's regime. He thought idly about the soccer pitches, wondering if and where Americans might play. He thought about his breakfast, which hadn't been too bad (except for the powdered eggs) and wondered what his next meal might look like. He also noted, in passing, that an awful lot of things at Abu Ghraib seemed to be named "Mortar-something."

Krump

Dizl didn't recognize the sound right away, perhaps because movies have made clichés of the sound and sight of explosions, their representations of hand grenades and mortar rounds exploding in fiery conflagrations the hero can leap away from at the last second. There was a microsecond's lag time between the noise and his reaction.

The first boom stunned Lunch Lady, catching him completely unprepared. "It stopped me in my tracks," he said. The sound came from in front of him; he figured the round probably landed outside of the base near the apartments outside the west wall. At the time he had no idea how to gauge how close the blast was and still had expectations of balls of fire billowing into the sky à la Hollywood. An instant later he witnessed the second blast. It all felt like slow motion; it looked as if the mortar had hit the top of the western wall. While the lieutenant did not see the anticipated fireball, he did see debris fly outwards and upward from the wall. The sight finally triggered his motion.

Oh right! That's a mortar, Dizl thought and began to run too.

The only available direction was back to where he had started from, so he hauled ass that way. He could hear the hiss as the rockets passed overhead and the sound of more explosions in the direction of the helo pad. He had arrived at a wall made of cement blocks standing perhaps twelve feet high, and Dizl recognized it after a moment as the one he'd passed on his way to breakfast. Just on the other side of the wall was the Mortar Café, the guys from Maine, his new home.

Great! I made it, he thought, stopping to catch his breath. When he looked up, Dizl was face to face with a large sign: FUEL POINT. He was standing next to thousands and thousands of gallons of fuel: volatile, inflammable, explosive fuel.

ShitShitShitShit, he thought and took off running again, knowing that if a mortar hit the fuel point (and surely it's what the bastards were aiming for?), he wouldn't survive.

Lunch Lady had seen the sign too and was also running while holding a similar internal conversation about the explosive potential of all that gas and diesel. The full realization of the situation struck him most forcefully when the oldest guy in the platoon went bolting past him as if he were standing still.

"My pace did not pick up until Thorndike flew past me in a sprint toward safety," he recalled later. "Thinking this was a good idea, I joined him running as fast as I could."

They arrived back at the Mortar Café more or less at the same moment, bursting through the door and into the illusory shelter of their dwelling place.

Krump. Krump. Two more shells touched down outside, more unwelcome gifts from the local insurgents.

Some of the other guys were in there—Parker, Turtle, the big kid they called Humpty, wide-eyed Lost Boys with their hands held over their ears and their mouths open. Dizl couldn't bring himself to tell them about the ocean of fuel that lay not twenty-five yards away from the cinder blocks against which several of them rested their trusting backs. Later, they would put sandbags on the windows and lobby the leadership to get the gasoline moved a little farther away.

The Mainers' baptism by mortar fire removed any vestige of denial about the dangers of the place and situation that Dizl, Lunch Lady, Skeletor, Turtle, and the rest of the Lost Boys had been brought to serve in.

Later, after his friend Wendy sent him the novel *Life of Pi*, Dizl was able to articulate what his first day at FOBAG had shown him: *I'm in a rowboat with a fucking tiger, and all around me is ocean. The tiger is under the tarp. I can't see it, but it's there. And there's nothing I can do about it.*

On his first evening's duty in Tower 7–1, listening to the still-strange sound of the muezzin calling the faithful to prayer from the nearby mosque, Private Dizl was startled when a *hamama*, a pigeon the size of a large duck, blundered into the side of his tower with a hollow *thunk*.

It fell, flapping dismally, just inside the wire.

Hey, thought Dizl, with a Mainer's reflexive recognition of a chance to do a little living off the land. *That thing would taste good roasted.*

All of a sudden, an Iraqi kid materialized beside the wire, obviously with the same thought in mind. He peered up at Dizl and pointed inquiringly in the direction of the bird's carcass.

"No," Dizl said initially. Then, curious to see what the kid did next, he relented. "OK why not? You can have it."

The kid grabbed the pigeon and disappeared into a tent. Soon enough, the appetizing aroma of roasting hamama reached Dizl's nostrils for the first time, which told Dizl that detainees had means of building fires in their tents.

That was an eye-opener.

He would later come to find that at least one group of detainees had turned a corner of their tent into a little blacksmith's shop for the express purpose of manufacturing shivs, shanks, and even swords out of scrap metal and rebar. Material wasn't nearly as difficult to come by as one might think. Ganci was built on a landfill. When the detainees were feeling energetic, they could dig straight down and find all sorts of materials and scrap.

Dizl had worked as a guard at the Maine State Prison, where prisoners were also known to do some creative repurposing. They made everything from knives to bongs to slingshots and crossbows and all other manner of contraband out of only what pieces were available to them. So the ingenuity of the detainees at Abu Ghraib was not as surprising to Dizl as it would be to some.

Aside from the mortars, it was in the area of basic hygiene that life at Abu Ghraib departed most dramatically from any American norm. There were primitive shower points and a whole lot of porta-potties, which were generally filled to capacity or beyond and stank like nothing Dizl had ever encountered before. There was also trash on the ground—a lot of it.

You've got fifteen-year-olds . . . and over there's a ninety-year-old man . . . so how are we doing the control, care, and treatment for these two very different sorts of prisoners? How can we possibly be meeting their different needs?

Overall, Dizl thought, there was something slapdash and contingent about Abu Ghraib. It reminded him less of a functioning detention center than of a semi-successful refugee camp thrown up in the first few weeks after a disaster. Walking into the 'Ghraib was like something out of *The Lord of the Rings* mixed with *Lord of the Flies,* and it reminded Dizl of a Hieronymus Bosch painting of hell.

"Calling FOBAG a prison would be like selling apricots at a peach stand," Dizl explained. "Sure, there are similarities, but an apricot isn't a peach."

But the Americans had been at Abu Ghraib for months, not weeks, and UNICEF was not en route. In fact, once their headquarters in Baghdad had been strategically bombed in the initial round of insurgent attacks, the United Nations itself had pulled out of Iraq.

Brigadier General Janis Karpinski would later quote a general, roaring "We're running a prison system for an entire country by the seat of our pants!"[5] That's how it felt to Private Thorndike, too.

We're not meeting these people's needs. And we're still making this up as we go along.

Dizl was alone in an end tower one night. His back was to the village of Nasser Wa Salam. The proximity of the village meant there was a history of sniper fire coming from the people who lived right on the other side of the wall, so sniper screens hung over the little window. They'd have to sit with their backs to the snipers, concentrating on their areas of responsibility. Sometimes their duty included ignoring the impact of bullets on the sandbags behind them as the Iraqis tried to shoot through the peephole opening.

---

5 Ricks, *Fiasco,* 204.

Dizl looked around and estimated that between the village in back and the detainees in front, he had about thirty feet of what anyone could really call friendly space.

In front of him, by the shower point, a faucet dribbled water. Periodically, as Dizl watched, someone would come along, use the stinking porta-potty, then come to the faucet to wash his feet for prayer. Then someone else would come along and fill a plastic water bottle.

Hold on. This isn't good, Dizl would think.

Looking around, Dizl saw a detainee of perhaps sixty seated nearby. He bore a strong likeness to one of Dizl's high school math teachers—a smart man, but really, really depressed.

"Hey!" said Dizl, pointing to the water. "Look, the way those men are using that water is no good. *Mushkallah!* Not safe."

The man looked up. In impeccable English, he answered, "Yes. I am a doctor. My specialty is in internal medicine."

Dizl regarded him with astonishment.

"Although I work on hearts." The doctor continued. "Cardiology. You understand?"

"Sure, but . . ."

"Yes. Well, don't worry, mister. These men . . . their immune systems will simply . . . well, they will have to tolerate this." He made a gesture with his hands that encompassed the tap, the porta-potties, and perhaps the whole of Abu Ghraib. "What else can one do?"

It wasn't a cop-out, Dizl realized. It was simple reality. The detainees had to urinate and defecate. The porta-potties were overflowing. They had to wash their feet. They had to drink water. There was one water source. They were stuck at Abu Ghraib. What else can one do?

Dizl sat back in his seat.

He thought about the depressed heart doctor, the roasting hamama, about the old man shuffling along, leaning on a young boy. He thought about the mortars and the meager protection of the Mortar

Café, and then compared that with the stark absence of protection afforded to the detainees living in canvas tents behind wire fences.

After a few hours of mind-numbing boredom, Dizl heard the sound of boots coming up the stairs. A helmet bearing the full-bird insignia of a colonel appeared through the floor. Private Thorndike leaped immediately to attention.

Colonel David E. Quantock was the newly appointed brigade commander for the Sixteenth MP Brigade under which the 152nd served at Abu Ghraib. He was making what the troops would soon learn were frequent evening rounds of the posts and areas of operations (AOs) throughout Abu Ghraib.

Once he had put the soldier at ease, as only a commanding officer can do, Colonel Quantock turned his gaze outward.

"So, Private Thorndike," he said. "What do you think?"

"About Abu Ghraib, sir?"

"About Abu Ghraib."

It is hard to explain what it's like being a junior ranking enlisted soldier having a conversation with a full-bird colonel. He is, essentially, your boss's boss's boss, who has the power not only to put you in prison for speaking to him the wrong way, if he so chooses, but he can also order you to your certain death.

In addition, anything one says to a high-ranking commissioned officer is bound to work its way back down through the chain of command where it acts as an excuse for your noncommissioned officer to give you an ass chewing for "jumping the chain of command." And no, it does not matter that the colonel came to you asking you questions.

"Well, sir," said Dizl. "It strikes me that this place is something like a cross between a refugee camp and a prison, and frankly, whatever it is, it's just not sustainable."

"Go on," said Quantock.

Emboldened, Dizl went on: "I've worked in a prison, sir. I know what a functioning prison looks like, and this isn't it."

"Uh huh."

"The hardest part is going to be teaching our guys the job, teaching them how to do custody and control. Even if you've had the training, it's a difficult job, and they haven't had the training. If anything, because they're field artillery, they've had the opposite class—how to kill people. And killing people isn't that hard when you're in the middle of a war zone, scared shitless. Sir."

"Go on," said Quantock.

Dizl looked inquiringly at him, but the colonel evidently meant it.

"OK, in theory these detainees are all terrorists, right? They're all our enemy. That old guy, that kid, that poor bastard there who used to be a doctor, if they got hold of some weapons, we would be facing an in-house insurgency and we would have no choice: We would have to shoot them."

"Yes."

"Since you asked, sir, I think the whole place really needs to be completely reorganized," said Dizl firmly. "And preferably with Maslow's hierarchy of needs in mind."

"Maslow's hierarchy of needs," the colonel repeated.

With characteristic enthusiasm, Dizl explained.

Abraham Maslow was a humanistic psychologist who developed a theory of personality that became influential in a variety of spheres—education, to name an obvious one, but also corrections. In Maslow's hierarchy, basic physiological needs such as food, water, the ability to maintain a consistent body temperature, and safety are necessities for basic human functioning.

"We have placed these people in a situation in which their basic needs are not being met, and those unsatisfied needs are going to control their thoughts and behaviors. This isn't good, sir."

Dizl went on for a while. Quantock was a good listener, and perhaps it was pleasant for the colonel to spend time discussing ideas with another middle-aged man, one whose years made him a peer even as his low rank removed him from the realm of commissioned officers whose words might be tinted by ambition or slanted for the time-honored purpose of covering their ass.

At last, Colonel Quantock got to his feet. He bade the soldier a grave and courteous farewell and departed. What Dizl didn't know was that the colonel was on one of his usual trips out to the "front lines." Quantock's AO covered thousands of square miles and he had four brigades under his command. Over the course of the next year or so, the man would log more than one hundred thousand miles on his vehicle getting out to see his troops.

President Bush insisted that morale among troops in Iraq was much higher than people back home thought, "just ask people who have been there." But it quickly became clear to anyone who actually did that soldiers in Iraq, particularly those in the National Guard and reserve units, were very unhappy: "Many soldiers described their training as insufficient. . . . A survey of twelve hundred deployed soldiers from the Illinois Army National Guard found that 'the majority of soldiers feel they are poorly informed, inadequately cared for, and that training in their units is boring and unorganized,' according to a summery by Brigadier General Charles Fleming, the deputy commander of the Illinois Guard."[6]

Colonel Quantock's goal was to get out to the troops and tell them from his own lips why their jobs guarding the detainees were so important. It was his belief that if his soldiers knew why they were doing something, they would most often get behind it.

"You can't just give an order and say, 'because I said so,'" Quantock said. "If it doesn't work with my kids, it won't work with soldiers."

The next morning, Captain Trevino accosted Dizl: "What on earth did you say to Quantock?" Trevino inquired.

"What are you talking about, sir?"

---

6 Ricks, *Fiasco*, 309.

"Today, in the Command Staff Meeting, Quantock told us he had a long conversation last night with a certain Private Thorndike . . ."

"Oh, shit, sir, really?"

". . . about the condition of the facility. He said we all needed to get on board with what you were talking about. What were you talking about?"

"Maslow's hierarchy of needs," said Dizl, and he set about explaining the philosophy to his Captain.

As it turned out, Dizl had made quite an impression on the colonel. His philosophy, and the philosophy of the Mainers regarding the treatment and humane housing of detainees, would filter out from Quantock to the other units at the 'Ghraib. While official US policy was "hands off" in light of the allegations surrounding the 372nd, it was Dizl and the Mainers, combined with Quantock's own leadership philosophies, that began pushing detainee operations in the morally righteous (or as close as one can get in a war zone) direction.

Not long after the First Platoon had begun working in Ganci, Specialist Cohen, the twenty-seven-year-old father of two little girls, arrived at Abu Ghraib to fill a hole in the roster left vacant when a soldier scheduled to be deployed got sick.

The new man was assigned to Tower G-7-1. Each of the guard towers overlooking Ganci was composed of a wooden, sand-filled box measuring roughly ten feet by ten feet, with a wooden, sand-filled roof overhead draped in anti-sniper netting. This structure rested upon a metal conex box, which looked like a shipping container one might see stacked on a wharf in Baltimore, or piled like enormous Legos in a Kuwaiti desert. Specialist Cohen and Dizl would be standing watch back to back for one twelve-hour watch after another, noon to midnight, for months to come.

Dizl set about getting the new guy oriented and up to speed. First, he gave a comprehensive overview of the situation on the ground: "Pretty much FUBAR, so trust in the leadership and, as Huladog would say, 'remember the three-hour rule.'"

"And listen, Specialist Cohen. What is your handle going to be for talking on the radio?"

By this time, the rest of the soldiers of the 152nd already had their nicknames. The peer-bestowed branding worked out well enough for some: Skeletor, Tex, Red, and Knight Ranger were all cool names. Others, however—Dizl, Turtle, Beerboy, and Lunch Lady—had to live with their goofy call signs.

As he considered the question, Specialist Cohen began rolling up his pant leg. Glowering from his calf muscle, he had a tattoo of the comic book character Wolverine.

"I was thinking, maybe, Wolverine?" he said insecurely.

"Well," said Dizl thoughtfully. "That would be pretty cool as a cool-guy name. Of course, the guys in my platoon stuck me with Dizl."

"Dizl?"

"You know," Kelly said, a Mainer doing an absentminded impression of Snoop Dogg, "ThornDizl-mantizzle dog word up ham slice . . . whatever."

They laughed.

A call came over the little radio. "Does anyone have any sugar? We made coffee in the command post, and can't find sugar to put into it."

"I have some," Specialist Cohen volunteered. "I've got a bunch in my rucksack."

"We have sugar here in 7-1," Dizl reported.

"Right on!" squawked one voice.

Another barked, "Who's got sugar?"

"The new guy," said Dizl.

"What's his call sign?" asked Huladog.

Dizl looked at Specialist Cohen, still sitting there with his pant leg rolled up. Dizl smiled.

"Sugar," he said. "The new guy's name is *Sugar!*"

Sugar jumped to his feet. "You bastard!" he protested, reaching for the radio, but it was too late. The news was out. *New guy calls himself Sugar. Ain't that sweet?*

Shortly after arriving, Sugar went to assist Turtle in handling an injured detainee; he prepared to don latex gloves as per the SOP, to minimize the potential for germs to be transferred to or from the prisoner.

"You won't need those," said Turtle.

"What do you mean? We have to wear gloves."

"Trust me."

The new MP didn't trust Turtle and put the gloves on his hands. Within seconds, the gloves began to swell as the latex trapped the perspiration continuously exuding from his wrists and palms. Within minutes Sugar had a set of watery udders dangling at the ends of his arms. The detainees, including the injured one, found it very entertaining.

A man could drink twelve liters of water every day and never need to pee. They drank Turkish bottled water until summer came and the heat got hotter. Then the Turkish water became foggy and had sea monkeys swimming in it. The men were ordered not to drink it. The lab at Camp Victory in Baghdad tested it and, unsurprisingly, it was found to be non-potable, having traces of diesel fuel, feces of unknown origin, pesticides, and other contaminants.

The order was given: "Whatever you do, don't drink the water with the purple label!"

No wait: "FRAGO! Don't drink the water with the blue label. The purple label's fine."

Because it was hot, and they were thirsty, some guys got fed up with the confusion and drank whatever water came their way. So

Dizl started a rumor that the terrorists had put semen in the blue-labeled bottles along with all the other crap. This at least kept the Lost Boys from drinking it.

Eventually, a better product, or at least ones containing no visible life-forms, replaced the bad water. The ground at Abu Ghraib as, indeed, all over Iraq, was littered with plastic bottles. When they come to excavate this ancient land, archaeologists of the future will find, amid the old news of bones, teeth, and scraps of sharpened metal, the plastics that will alone declare this to have been a more modern violence.

SIX

WHY?

"[The Iraqi Shiites are] the insurmountable obstacle."
—Abu Musab al-Zarqawi, leader of Al-Qaeda in Iraq,
in a letter to Osama bin Laden

"MY BIGGEST REGRET of my life is becoming a statistic of Abu Ghraib Prison, Iraq," Dizl said, years after returning home "safe and sound."

He was riding the ferry home to North Haven one afternoon when he found himself in a conversation about the war in Iraq, and his time there, with a woman he knew in the way all Mainers seem to know each other.

"Why were you in Iraq?" she asked.

"My country sent me," Dizl replied.

"Do you regret going?"

"No."

"What did you do there?"

"My unit replaced the picture takers at Abu Ghraib."

"Did you get injured?"

"Yes, I was blown up, and received a moderate TBI."

"We should just bring all our troops home, and let them just kill themselves."

"We can't, remember September 11? Al-Qaeda will do that again."

"Would you go back?"

"Yes, I would."

"Is it all really worth it?"

Dizl pondered for a moment before answering. Not because he didn't have an answer, but because his experience told him that if he stood up for what he believed in, people would become uncomfortable, exclusionary, and discriminating

"Ask any family member of someone who was murdered on September 11 if it's all worth it."

They talked about politics, and he explained that the Taliban is Afghanistan's problem, and that we are after al-Qaeda. He asked her to try and imagine North Haven Island suddenly being populated by a thousand Republicans. Her eyes got big as she exclaimed, *"Oh, God!"*

His antianxiety meds are designed to help Dizl coexist with people like the nurse from the ferry, or any number of the American populace who aren't bothered by their own apathy and ignorance.

Dizl gets criticized for not going to basketball games on the island. He can't go because the cheering people remind him of thousands of screaming detainees that were being slaughtered by insurgent mortars, and of a man being brought to the base of his tower by his family. The dying man continued hemorrhaging blood as they begged Dizl to help him. Dizl can't forget the man gasping like a fish on the ice, his eyes bulging wide as he looked up at Dizl and died. The dead man's family still glares at the retired soldier in his dreams, as if somehow haunting Dizl for the murder of their loved one.

"We had no stuff," he tells his nightmares in desperation. "We were surrounded. I begged, borrowed, or stole any lifesaving tools that I could get my hands on."

To this day, if Dizl shares this truth with people, they think he's crazy. "Oh poor dear," they say. "He's just too intense; let's not invite them to dinner. Just knowing is too much for me."

They don't care that when Dizl goes to bed at night, he has no tangible sense of what he did that day; TBI and PTSD threw a real kink in his short-term memory. The truth is, Dizl never really left Abu Ghraib. He brought a piece of Maine there, and then turned around and brought a piece of that terrible place home with him to roost.

The Islamic faith, to which virtually all Iraqis subscribe, traces its origins to the early seventh-century life and ministry of the Prophet Muhammad. The Prophet was born sometime around the end of the sixth century, and by the time he died in 632 he had conquered most of Arabia. He had, unfortunately, failed to clearly nominate a successor.

Within the first decades, therefore, a power struggle had erupted between those who wanted Islam to be led by a *khalif* (Arabic for "successor," and rendered in English as "caliph") and those who believed that the leadership should descend through the biological line of the Prophet traced through Ali, husband to Muhammad's beloved daughter Fatima. The competition between these two groups quickly turned violent, and much of the violence played out within the territory of what is now known as Iraq, which had first fallen under the dominion of Islam in 633.

Imam Ali, the Prophet's son-in-law, dwelled in Iraq and was assassinated there. As per Ali's instructions, his followers strapped his body to a white camel and buried him where the camel stopped; this site became the holy city of Najaf.

Hussein, the son of Ali and the grandson of the Prophet, was killed, or "martyred," by the superior forces of the Caliphate near Kerbala.

Thus in 2004, when Al-Qaeda in Iraq—a Sunni group—detonated a series of car and suicide bombs in Kerbala and Baghdad that killed hundreds, the victims were Shiite pilgrims gathering in ritual mourning for the death of Hussein ibn Ali. And when the violence in present-day Iraq is met with disgusted explanations along the lines of "these people have been killing each other for centuries," this is what they are talking about.

Tempting though it is to declare the ancient Sunni/Shiite divide a permanent obstacle to cooperation and peace among Muslims, it should be said that religious animosity could be intensified, or even created, by political rivalries in which goods other than theological correctness are at stake.

Protestants and Catholics fought bitter, horrendously violent wars against each other, and not only in the far distant past but more recently, as seen in Northern Ireland. At the same time, people have been known to omit even foundational theological disagreements and cooperate nicely when it is in both of their interests or those of external, dominant powers.

Faith, in other words, can prove interchangeable and malleable when profitable. Unfortunately, religious identity in the Iraq of 2004 had become a hard bright line that fewer and fewer Iraqi citizens could bring themselves to cross.

Saddam Hussein was a Sunni and his Baath Party was likewise predominantly Sunni. Afghanistan is largely Sunni, with the Taliban representing the fundamentalist end of the Sunni spectrum. Osama bin Laden and al-Qaeda are offshoots of the Sunni fundamentalist Wahabi movement in Saudi Arabia.

In 1979, Wahabis took over the Grand Mosque in Mecca, trapping thousands of worshippers and provoking a siege and final battle in which hundreds died, but the American public, riveted by the Iranian hostage crisis playing out at the same time, paid little attention to this cataclysmic event.

This was unfortunate; "the siege of Mecca" would prove the beginning of our problems with bin Laden and al-Qaeda. The insurgent group Al-Qaeda in Iraq that sprang up in the aftermath of the invasion, and its leader, al-Zarqawi, are also Sunnis and boast a far higher proportion of foreign—especially Saudi—fighters as well.

In neighboring Iran the overwhelming majority are Shiites—estimates put the percentage at 90–95. With 63 percent of the total, Shiites make up a smaller majority in Iraq, with the remainder of the populace composed of Sunni Arabs, Kurds, and a sprinkling of Christians. Despite their greater numbers, the Sunnis have politically and socially dominated Iraqi Shiites in part due to the fact that the Sunnis were favored by the British during the period of British colonial rule, and afterward they enjoyed the de facto support of the United States and Western Europe.

Political power tends to translate into economic power, and Iraq's Sunnis have reaped the associated benefits of better nutrition, housing, health care, and education, making them seem more familiar to Westerners.

Knowing just this much, one might begin to understand why a nation weakened by years of political repression and misrule; two disastrous, bloody wars; a decade of sanctions; and the chaos, disorder, and violence that followed the American invasion could so easily slide into the prepared grooves of sectarian revenge, power struggles, and cyclical violence.

One can tidy up the situation the Mainers walked into in 2004 to 2005, with its jumbled names of cities, militias, and battles, by imagining a very rough line drawn between north and south. In the north there was a Sunni majority: al-Qaeda, al-Zarqawi, Fallujah,

Mosul, and Anbar Province. Shiite groups, Kerbala, Najaf, Nasseria, Muqtada al-Sadr, and the Sadr Militia operated to the south.

Smack in the disputed center is the capital, Baghdad, and its hapless satellite, Abu Ghraib.

When the Mainers arrived in Iraq, they knew little or nothing about Islam. But in this, they were no different from the majority of Americans, for whom Islam is as mysterious (and perhaps as frightening) as Christianity doubtless appears to an Iraqi. While a bit of cultural sensitivity training formed part of the anxious little mini-education stuffed in at Camp Victory, soldiers and detainees would learn most of what they would ever know of their respective characters and cultures from each other.

The gulf that separated the Mainers' and detainees' respective understanding of what was happening at Abu Ghraib made itself clear in a conversation Red had with a group in Ganci 7 in the days that followed the first mass casualty attack in April. Having mustered their courage and best English vocabulary, they demanded, "Mister-mister, why are you doing this to us?"

After a short, mutually bewildering back-and-forth, it emerged that these detainees had reached the conclusion that it was the Americans, or their Coalition Partners, who were mortaring Abu Ghraib.

That is, since the Americans had taken the Iraqis into custody because they thought they were bad, it followed that they had been brought to Abu Ghraib to be concentrated into dense groups and bombed out of existence.

The fact that, as Red pointed out, American soldiers were also being injured and killed by the mortars wasn't persuasive. Perhaps they had learned to judge brutality by the "what would Saddam do?" standard, and assumed Americans also believed that committing mass murder was simply routine politics.

On the other hand, perhaps their interpretation was based on the worldwide public image of the United States—the rhetoric President

Bush and past presidents pushed to the world that the United States is the world's only superpower, a nation of unlimited resources and astonishing power.

Our psychological operations had done a fantastic job reinforcing this message to the people of Iraq, especially when it preceded the undeniably unmatched might of the US military. Ipso facto, Americans can do whatever we want to do, and it follows that if we don't do something it is because we have chosen not to. When our troops didn't prevent the looting of Iraq's treasures, protect pilgrims at holy sites from mass murder, or house detainees in decent, safe, and hygienic facilities, it stood to reason in the detainees' minds that their harrowing experiences in Abu Ghraib were all part of a carefully orchestrated American plot.

In processing, where detainees and their guards met for the first time, there was nothing done to alleviate the mutual incomprehension. It started with a captured Iraqi being informed—via an unvetted interpreter—that they were being sent to Abu Ghraib. To the average Iraqi, this was akin to a citizen of the Soviet Union being informed that they were going to the Gulag.

For similar reasons, not even the most pro-Coalition Iraqi could possibly drive in through the gates of Abu Ghraib feeling optimistic about his prospects, and none of what he saw within its walls would soothe him.

Specialist Yogi met new arrivals at the low building bearing a sign reading "391st Military Police Battalion Detainee Inprocessing." It was a tidy white sign, decorated with reproductions of the shoulder patches worn by airborne and MP units in charge, but its effect was somewhat spoiled by the words "Prisoner Inprocessing," which had earlier been spray-painted in large black and, unfortunately, permanent letters on the gritty concrete wall.

The wall itself was cracked and battered; large chunks were missing as if some giant toddler had been teething on the concrete. Wires looped, snakelike, from eyebolt to eyebolt before disappearing behind a doorframe. Was it age, looting, or gunfire that knocked off patches of the cement cladding? What were the wires draped across the building and disappearing through the doors going to be used for?

Original windows had been covered over with plywood, and two plywood doors marked PRISONER ENTRY and VISITORS were flanked by makeshift benches made out of boards resting on stacked concrete blocks. There was one battered, plastic garbage can and an air conditioning unit with its tangled wire snaking through a gap cut into the visitor's doorframe.

Meanwhile, Yogi had been told he could assume the men presented to him at inprocessing (in groups numbering as many as 125 at a time) were fighters, insurgents, or head-choppers, any one or more of whom might just have made a personal decision that very morning to kill as many Americans as possible before taking the express route from Abu Ghraib to Paradise.

Surely this was true for at least some of the men and women who walked through those doors, and all of them looked the part. Meanwhile, presumably, the Iraqis could do the math as easily as he could: Yogi drove the bus from inprocessing to Ganci alone, outnumbered by the prisoners one hundred (or more) to one. No other soldiers rode the bus with him, not even a single ally who might've sat, facing backward, to keep an eye on the passengers while he drove.

"There were never enough of us," Dizl would say, "never enough of the right people. So we had to become the right people. We had to make ourselves enough."

On one occasion, when the descriptions of the group waiting for him at inprocessing were especially hair-raising, Yogi decided a bit of theater was called for.

All the Mainers kept a bottle of hand sanitizer tucked into a helmet-strap, in the hope that frequent use would keep pathogens at bay. Yogi gave his helmet a generous coating of the stuff.

Hand sanitizer is mostly alcohol, and thus it's flammable. Yogi paused briefly outside the room where the incoming detainees awaited him, lit his helmet on fire, and burst through the doors.

"Welcome to hell, my friends. Time to learn the rules!"

Other times, Yogi and Skeletor were assigned to be "mobile rovers." It was their job to patrol the perimeters of the compounds looking for fights, suspicious activity, and breaches in the concertina wire. They were also to serve as backup to the other mobile rovers in adjacent compounds. Periodically they also manned a tower for a comrade who needed to hit the head or sneak a smoke.

As a mobile rover, one of Yogi's more exciting responsibilities was to perform the headcounts in Gancis 7 and 8. This meant stripping off body armor and gun belt and entering a compound through the double gates of the "shark cage" carrying nothing but a pen and a clipboard.

The hundreds of detainees would line up in front of him. Stepping forward one by one, they would present their wristband for Yogi's inspection. The bands looked something like a hospital identity bracelet and they displayed a small photograph of the detainee together with his eleven-digit identification number. Yogi would match the number to the name on his list, check that the photo resembled its wearer, and make appropriate notations.

Count was often the time when Yogi would be told of minor medical problems or other needs, and sometimes news of a planned riot or other dangerous activity would be mumbled beneath the breath of a detainee, his face kept carefully blank.

Yogi had received virtually no training in any of this. Indeed, on the first day that he entered Ganci 8 to perform his first Count, no one had thought to tell him that Ganci 8 was reserved primarily for detainees strongly suspected of being Fedayeen: the trained, loyal, and angry remnants of the paramilitary organization created by Saddam.

When Yogi—sans armor, sans weapon—entered the compound, he found himself swiftly encircled by detainees, their eyes and body language transmitting enough hostility to make the hot air crackle.

Yogi beat a tactical retreat to return later with reinforcements. Count was completed, but it was a disquieting experience. After all, it was plain that there weren't enough MPs available to have reinforcements for every Count (which guards had to complete three times per shift).

"I can help you with this," declared a short, wiry, utterly self-confident Marine, when the problem was discussed over dinner in the chow hall that evening.

"Do you smoke?"

"Yes," said Yogi.

"This is what you do," said the Marine, who had taken on the nickname Gunsmoke. "Tomorrow morning, you go into Ganci 8 just like you did today, all by yourself. Those Fedayeen form up around you again, if they start with the eye-fucking again, you just stand in front of the guy you figure to be the leader of the gang. And you light yourself a cigarette . . ."

"Yeah?"

". . . and hold it up in the air like this." Gunsmoke demonstrated, clamping a ballpoint between his second and third fingers so that it poked up in the air.

"All right," said Yogi skeptically. "But where are you going to be?"

"Don't worry about me. I'll be in the tower."

"Great. You'll be a hundred yards away."

"Just hold the cigarette up for . . . let's say ten seconds."

"10-4," said Yogi. "If you say so."

The next morning, Yogi went back to Ganci 8. He peeled off his body armor and weapons and let himself in through the shark cage. Again, he found himself surrounded by glowering men. With casual aplomb, Yogi pulled a cigarette out of the pack in his pocket, put it to his lips, and lit it. He took a good, deep lungful of smoke and then held the cigarette up above his right shoulder, as he had been instructed.

There was a very brief (far less than ten seconds) silence. Then the crack of a rifle, and a cloud of gritty dirt squirted up from the bare ground ahead of Yogi's boots.

Yogi brought his hand around and inspected what was left of the cigarette. It had been clipped off, very neatly, just above the point where the small white paper cylinder emerged from between his knuckles.

His eyes refocused beyond the amputated cigarette, and his cold blue gaze met and held the basilisk stare of the leader of these Fedayeen.

"Do we understand each other now?" he asked.

Further on in the deployment, Dizl gave Yogi and the others some pointers he'd picked up, having been trained as a prison guard and working in a high-risk "super" maximum-security prison.

"Vary your route and your routine," he advised, pointing out that people are much more habit driven than we think, and habit breeds predictability. "It's too easy to fall into a predictable routine, turning right at the command post door every morning, walking clockwise and then counterclockwise, day after day. Given that you eat at more or less the same times, it is normal for your body to declare itself ready for the Port-a-John with such reliable regularity that a detainee could set his watch by you, if he had one."

Dizl's insights were validated when, during a search of one of the detainee's tents, they found a piece of paper neatly charting the guard's names, their shifts, meals, bathroom breaks, and days off. Such information was invaluable when it came to the timing of such activities as transferring contraband, beating up a rival, or planning an escape.

When not on roving patrol, Dizl and the other soldiers were working in a guard tower. It was an activity similar to standing watch on an offshore scallop dragger or working a fire tower in the big North woods. The guy in the tower was tasked with keeping his eyes peeled for problems. Other people had the job of putting the fires out.

Ganci's fires were (usually) metaphorical, though they burned hot. When they weren't trying to dodge incoming mortar rounds, the detainees at Abu Ghraib did what any confined, bored group of humans will do: They invented social problems and then attempted to solve them. At least some of these solutions took violent forms; physical assaults were not uncommon.

The center towers, like Tower 7-1, had two seats in which two soldiers could sit back to back, one guy facing the sunrise, the other watching the sun set. They did this for fourteen hours a day, seven days a week. Sometimes they'd do this for weeks at a time before getting a day off to recover.

Tower 7-1 was nicknamed the Hawk's Nest because of the tactical and visually important position it held on the Ganci Compound grid. From there, a soldier could scan a 360-degree slice of the neighborhood: FOBAG proper, plus the dreaded overpass that loomed outside the westerly wall of the prison, so close they could read the road signs. The town of Nasser Wa Salam sat less than thirty yards from the nearest outside boundary of the northwest section of the compound. A good set of binoculars gave the man on watch the gist of what was happening in the general FOBAG vicinity. If a mortar or two came sailing in during daylight hours, a soldier in the Hawk's Nest could get a visual on where it had originated and landed, enabling the occupants of Ganci to respond more swiftly to whatever was coming next.

The two soldiers in the Hawk's Nest were each assigned to watch an east–west running lane, a path between the fences of the detainee pens. Parker and Dizl generally took turns covering the westerly side of Ganci 7-1. Sugar and Captain Morgan watched the easterly lane of Ganci 5-3—the lane that was Parker and Dizl's six o'clock.

"They had my six," is how Dizl describes this set-up. The phrase is claimed to have originated with fighter pilots unable to scan for any threat that might be directly behind the plane, but it has become a way to describe something deeper than mere "backup." You have to wait for backup, you don't have to wait for whoever has your six, they're already there; you don't even have check to make sure they're still there. You just know they are.

There was a kid in the 152nd nicknamed "Willard," a tall, twenty-ish, good-looking boy. Willard was scared of the mortars. Well, actually they were all scared of them. Only a moron wouldn't be. Willard's father was a chopper pilot for the Maine Air National Guard, and he flew into Kuwait to visit his son before the battalion crossed into Iraq. Because Willard's father had experience with medevac ("medical evacuation") flights, he knew too well what Willard was getting into. When the moment came, it was hard for father and son to say good-bye.

One morning, a few weeks (but numerous mortar attacks) after they had arrived at FOBAG, Willard seemed particularly anxious. Or maybe it was Dizl who was anxious and needed to offer encouraging words at least as much as Willard needed to hear them. In any event, Dizl took a large abdominal first-aid dressing out of his CLS (Combat Lifesaver) bag and wrote WILLARD on the front of it.

He showed it to the kid and said, "See? It's for you if you need it." He put it into his cargo pocket, and there it stayed. Whenever things got ugly, whenever the detainees seemed particularly grumpy, or a morning briefing contained yet another variation on the theme of "how we're gonna die today" (these were increasingly common as the insurgency increased in skill and ferocity), Dizl would catch Willard's eye and point to his pocket.

Within the confines of a civilian existence, it doesn't sound like it would be comforting. However, such morbid reassurances are common in places where the morbid is a daily occurrence. So it was normal in a world where the men of the 152nd would spend many moments asking their personal deities things like:

"Please, God, don't let me die here."

"Allah, don't let me get blown up by a mortar round, OK?"

"Buddha, could you please not let me be kidnapped and beheaded by insurgents who will broadcast my death for my mom to see on YouTube or LiveLeak?"

When Willard and Dizl would be separated for any length of time—for example when Willard was sent to Baghdad to provide security for a convoy—Dizl would greet their reunion with extravagant delight, hollering *"Willard!"* and hugging the boy until he blushed.

It was of great comfort to Willard to have the friendly giant Dizl covering his six, especially during the mortar attack of April 6, 2004. On Ganci Compound the detainees had taken a pretty severe hit, and they wondered if the all-powerful Americans were doing it or, if not, perhaps the Bad Guys on the outside were punishing them for getting too friendly with the infidel invaders?

Not surprisingly, within days of this first attack the detainees started to get pretty grumpy. Thousands of Iraqi men with rocks the size of softballs clenched in their scared and angry hands began loudly chanting their version of "Death to America."

Maybe they were hoping that if they chanted it loudly and sincerely enough, the insurgents on the outside would hear it, and spare the detainees another nightmarish assault. If so, within weeks it would be made agonizingly plain that their countrymen were not impressed.

On the other hand, the Americans took the detainees' words very seriously. In fact, the aggressive chanting would haunt dreams and echo in all similar sounds heard long after the Mainers went home. Dizl would hear it, an unbearable mnemonic, in the unified encouragements of crowds at high school basketball games or rock concerts:

Death to America!
Death to America!
Rah, rah, rah!

SEVEN

THE BROILER

"Why do we soldiers have to dig through local landfills for pieces of scrap metal and compromised ballistic glass to up-armor our vehicles?"

"As you know, you go to war with the army you have, not the army you might want or wish to have."

—Exchange between an American soldier
and Secretary of Defense Donald Rumsfeld

ONCE THE MEN of the 152nd settled into the routine of their deployment to Ganci, life began to take on a certain rhythmic predictability. At least it did for those whose responsibilities put them on the front lines with the detainees. When he was asked to come up with a "handle" for use when communicating, former Frito-Lay truck driver and now army specialist Shawn Keyte offered "Black Bear," with more hope than confidence. It didn't take.

The detainees had already christened him *Hesanoi*, which Keyte was told meant either "long, slender fruit" or "sheep herder." Though he had never had much to do with sheep, and did not think of himself as particularly fruit-like, the long, slender part was accurate.

Specialist Quint—a.k.a. Major Payne, the namesake and main character of his favorite movie—declared that Shawn reminded him of one of the old *Masters of the Universe* cartoon characters. So Shawn the truck driver became Skeletor to his fellow soldiers. The detainees, however, stuck with Hesanoi.

Major Payne had just spent several days renovating an old washroom in the Mortar Café into a first-class barbershop complete with camouflage netting to protect both barber and customer from the view of snipers and a repurposed, adjustable tank seat for the customer to sit on. He christened his new business the House O' Payne and, for a dollar, would clip hair according to military specifications. The dollar was put into a pot, to provide funding for a festive bash to be held when the tour of duty ended and the Mainers could go home.

But for those senior-ranking soldiers, such as Huladog, Beerboy, and Lunch Lady, whose pay grades granted them the dubious privilege of attending the military intelligence briefings, there was a growing unease. They did the best they could to shield the lower-ranking men of First Platoon from the more alarming bits of intel they were privy to, but the more experienced and perceptive among the men began to feel it nonetheless.

Sitting there, day after day in the Hawk's Nest, the sun hovering what felt like six inches above his head, Dizl watched the oncoming firestorm from the hot seat of the tower. He called it the Broiler.

It came on slowly. High-powered government representatives started showing up and taking walk-throughs to recon the situation on the ground. Any incident involving harm to a detainee not only had to be reported, but the report went straight up the chain of command to land on Rumsfeld's desk. Coming back down the chain of command was what seemed a constant stream of changes in the rules of engagement, even as the mortars fell and the command staffers looked grayer and more concerned by the day.

Dizl sat in his tower and watched as, outside the prison walls in the town of Abu Ghraib, Iraqi civilians were growing increasingly frustrated at the continued lack of basic services and the increasing rates of crime, along with the risks of being caught up in the growing violence. In March 2004, a mere 14 percent of Iraqis polled regarded the Coalition Provisional Authority with confidence, down from 47 percent only five months before.[7] ("This is America?" an Iraqi man said, despairing and disbelieving, to journalist Anthony Shadid. "We thought America could do anything."[8])

The heroic rescue of Jessica Lynch, as it had been told back in 2003, was publicly revealed to be another lie. And, of course, the photos from Abu Ghraib were about to become international headline news.

Dizl watched the frying pan heat up around him from his tower, his duty forcing him to sit powerless against the fury of the ever-burning Shemis (what the Americans took to calling Shamash, the Mesopotamian sun god) and watch the populace around him get angrier and the detainees become violently fidgety.

Sizzle, sizzle, my nizzle.

On Ashura, the holiest day of the year for Shia Muslims, nearly 180 people died when suicide bombers and cars laden with explosives detonated at shrines in Baghdad and Karbala.

Sizzle, sizzle went the Broiler, when four men from Blackwater Security were killed a few miles down the road in Fallujah. Their bodies had been burned, dragged behind a truck, and eventually hung from a bridge above the blue-green Euphrates. Dizl could see the smoke from the fires and the truckloads of insurgent fighters and weapons headed into the stronghold city.

In the Baghdad neighborhood known as Sadr City, the Mahdi Army ambushed a US Army patrol, killing eight Americans and wounding fifty-seven more. The Bad Guys weren't stupid. They could

---

7 Ricks, *Fiasco*, 326.
8 Anthony Shadid, *Night Draws Near* (New York: Picador, 2006).

see that the soldiers at Abu Ghraib were just so many fish in a barrel, inexperienced, underequipped, and undermanned. So the mortars splashed into everything and anyone, and the detainees got grumpy, and they picked up rocks from the ground within their enclosures and chanted "Death to America."

Messages from somewhere high up the chain came through loud, clear, and on repeat. The soldiers of the Sixteenth MP Brigade, the men and women from Maine, Ohio, Indiana, and Puerto Rico were not—repeat, *not*—to heap naked detainees into piles, force them to simulate fellatio, scare the piss or crap out of them, or otherwise do anything that remotely resembled those goddamned pictures. Don't take pictures of the detainees, and don't kill them.

Every day, the Lost Boys walked from their LSA to breakfast, and from breakfast to Ganci, where they passed a sign, red-on-white, Arabic and English, that was posted on the wire fence: WARNING THIS IS A RESTRICTED AREA. DEADLY FORCE IS AUTHORIZED. But actually, Dizl mused, the only people in the area with full authorization to use deadly force were the Bad Guys. The Americans had rules of engagement that were evolving from "defend yourself" to "you are accountable for every bullet. If you fuck up, you'll go to prison." Problem was, following the definition of "not fucking up" could get you killed.

Added to the stress of confusing ROEs, it was a tactical nightmare for the men stationed at the prison to defend it (or at least hide from the indirect fire, or IDF) because Abu Ghraib lay between two major highways, both primary transit routes for insurgent and coalition forces en route to and from various battle zones.

Baghdad was the city center from which Abu Ghraib and the insurgent stronghold of Fallujah were a mere fifteen miles to the north. So insurgents heading down to Sadr City, or up to Fallujah to prepare for or join in one of the cataclysmic battles there, would fire off a mortar round or toss a few grenades into Ganci compound as they passed by. When the insurgents decided to mount a sustained attack on Abu Ghraib—this became more common after the publication of the photos—the highways also provided elevated viewing platforms for spotters walking the mortar rounds into high-value targets.

The insurgent forces knew that the United States had a standing policy to avoid collateral damage wherever possible. So they learned that a ten-year-old boy made an excellent spotter for mortar fire, and that a VBIED driven behind a car filled with civilians bought itself time to get closer to the target. The son of a Maine game warden, recently returned from a tour in Iraq, said that al-Qaeda insurgents would use women as shields, shooting from behind their shoulders.

Not only did putting civilians in harm's way hinder our soldiers' ability to respond and give the insurgents a tactical advantage, it also gave them an edge in the back-and-forth propaganda war. Civilian deaths, from whatever cause, could be easily, ruthlessly "weaponized" against an occupation that claimed to be occupying Iraq for its own good. The more pictures the citizens of Iraq saw of women and children killed by allied forces, the less accepting they would be of continued occupation.

The IDF attacks on Ganci were inevitably going to kill and maim imprisoned Iraqis in far greater numbers than American soldiers, certainly many more than even the most brutal American MP would do. And yet Abu Ghraib received more mortar rounds after the photos were publicized, as if by blowing their own countrymen to pieces they were punishing the United States. Those infamous photos would fuel more deaths of both allied forces and Iraqi citizens.

Dizl's theory was that the Bad Guys were trying to get the detainees massed in Ganci to freak out and riot. The Americans would've had no choice but to rock them, and massacres would make more pictures to run on Al Jazeera.

The FOBAG rules of engagement did not allow for shooting a man standing on a highway overpass with binoculars and a cell phone, no matter how recognizable such behavior might be to soldiers who were, after all, trained in field artillery.

The insurgents were more than capable of figuring out the constraints under which the troops defending Abu Ghraib operated and exploiting these with eerie precision and flexibility. For example, one ROE would say something like, "You can only shoot a guy who is actually holding a weapon aimed at you. It is not enough to merely suspect him of having hostile intent: He has to be actually holding a gun."

Once insurgents figured out this rule, they would send a man who would appear on the roof of a building in full view of the Marine manning a perimeter tower. There, he would snatch up a rifle, obviously pre-positioned, aim, fire into the compound, then throw the rifle down. Marines preparing to return fire would watch as their opponent, now unarmed, dashed across the roof to the exit stairs, only to reappear minutes later on the roof of another building, where he would pluck up another pre-stashed rifle, aim it, and fire.

The detainees were sick of being detained under such conditions. *Who could blame them?* Dizl thought on more than one occasion. *You couldn't keep me penned in that mess for long either.* Meanwhile, it wasn't only the detainees who were wondering what the hell the world's only superpower was doing in and to Iraq. Operation Iraqi Freedom appeared to be headed south, if it had ever held to True North in the first place, which Dizl, among others, had begun to doubt.

The sun baked him in his armor and the rockets and the mortars kept falling, like a Biblical rain, on the just and the unjust alike. Taken all around, it was pretty fucking miserable.

EIGHT

SIEGE

"There are some who feel that the conditions are such that they can attack us there. My answer is 'Bring 'em on!' We've got the force necessary to deal with the security situation."

—President George W. Bush, July 2, 2003

WHILE A MAINER who enlisted in the National Guard in 2010 did so with the full knowledge that he or she would likely be deployed to Iraq or Afghanistan, someone like Skeletor, who joined the Guard in 1996, could be forgiven for assuming that he would be protecting the citizens of Maine during moments of statewide crisis. Or perhaps be sent to assist other states for a week or so, like to Louisiana during Hurricane Katrina.

In addition, employers of these guardsmen, like Frito-Lay or its parent company, PepsiCo, might also have presumed that if their truck driver had to change hats and become a guardsman for a time, his or her job wouldn't have to be held vacant for longer than a few weeks or, at most, a few months.

As it was, Skeletor was away from his Dexter-Dover-Fox-croft-Greenville route for sixteen months. PepsiCo was very nice about it. They sent Skeletor an enormous care package full of food, to fatten him up perhaps, or just to remind him of home.

The significance of food can easily be missed in the superabundance that passes for normal American life, but for the detained of Abu Ghraib as well as for their guards, a meal was not only nourishment but a source of entertainment, a means of demonstrating power, or a precious link to cultural identity, not to mention the only reliable relief from the otherwise boring sameness of the hours that pass behind the wire.

It was a food riot that had led to the seven detainees being taken to the Hard Site where Graner and England waited. Food's significance became dramatically obvious, too, when Abu Ghraib came under siege by the insurgents in the spring of the 152nd's deployment.

On April 9, Dizl wrote a letter to a friend back home. It was terse and to the point: "We're surrounded and under siege. Things don't look good. If I don't make it back, could you please take care of my hunting dogs for me? I don't want to leave my wife with that problem."

Dizl dropped it off in the mailbox at the company command post. He saw it as a bit of a Hail Mary; if Abu Ghraib "went Alamo," the chances were pretty good that the mail would not be delivered, but it made him feel better anyway.

Dizl wasn't the only one hedging his bets: Huladog received a number of envelopes containing last letters to wives and sweethearts, which he was requested to hold, just in case.

The First Sergeant, like the rest of Abu Ghraib's command staffers, did his best to shield the enlisted guys from knowing just how bad the situation was. The darkening under Hula's eyes and the thousand-yard stare told the men the truth.

To impose a siege on any FOB in Iraq essentially meant blowing up the trucks of everything from computer equipment to ordnance to water that traveled to and from the coalition's bases. Foreign workers, including American civilians who had signed up to work for the fabulous salaries offered by KBR/Halliburton, drove most of these trucks.

The trucks were arriving with less frequency the longer the 152nd stayed there, Dizl noticed. When the shit trucks had stopped coming to pump out the overflowing shitters, the story was that insurgents had kidnapped the KBR drivers and left their beheaded bodies inside the tanks of human waste.

Despite the US military's warning that Iraq's roads were far too dangerous for any traffic, a convoy of nineteen KBR trucks headed for Baghdad on the morning of April 9. It was attacked just outside of Abu Ghraib in what was the single deadliest incident involving US contractors in the war to that point. Six drivers died, another was kidnapped, and one simply vanished, never to be heard from again, while the rest sustained serious injuries. The billowing flames and black smoke were visible from Abu Ghraib, and the story arrived by the end of the day.

Dizl could only watch from his tower as an estimated eight hundred to one thousand fighters surrounded the prison. Buses and truckloads of insurgents were moving into the town, and once the fighters had unloaded themselves and their gear, women and children boarded and were driven away. The neighborhood around the prison fell eerily quiet as it became less of a town and more of a stronghold for the enemy forces.

At the time, the prison housed somewhere between seven and ten thousand detainees in Ganci alone. Thirty MPs managed these thousands on two twelve-hour watches, noon to midnight (Dizl's watch) and midnight to noon.

There were not enough soldiers to maintain control under optimal conditions, let alone while under a serious and sustained attack. Moreover, the besieged of FOBAG had been given a two-hour "standalone order," meaning that the soldiers there should expect no assistance from the outside for at least that long if they were assaulted by a large force. Everyone knew that there would not be anything like enough boots on the ground to hold Abu Ghraib for two hours. When the story of what had happened to the KBR convoy reached them, they watched the plume of smoke rising from nearby and wondered if they were about to share the fate of the kidnapped KBR driver.

"Save your last bullet for yourself" became one of the mottos among the Lost Boys.

As darkness set in, the inhabitants of FOBAG prepared for another uneasy night. Dizl and Sugar took up their posts in the tower overlooking Ganci 7.

"Hey Sugar," said Dizl.

"Yeah?"

"It's my little boy's birthday today."

"No kidding? April 9? Hey," Sugar said kindly. "Cool!"

"Listen, if I'm killed tonight, before midnight, could you make sure First Sergeant records the death date as the tenth instead?"

Sugar said, "Sure, Diz. Yes. I'll do that."

"Thanks," Dizl said. He felt a sense of relief like after he'd ensured the proper care of his hunting dogs.

There was more relief to come that night: Instead of the anticipated cry of artillery rounds sailing in over the walls or an insurgent assault they probably would not have been able to withstand, the denizens of Abu Ghraib heard the far-off purr of turbine engines. An Abrams tank and a Bradley fighting vehicle arrived. The Americans cheered the cheers of the liberated and the detainees joined in.

No shots were fired. The Bad Guys melted away into the night.

Even with the arrival of Marine and Army units offering protection, FOBAG remained under siege. Days passed, then a week. Between the chaos erupting in Baghdad and the violence up the road in Fallujah, coalition forces virtually everywhere in Iraq were busy with their own versions of the same problems. They didn't have enough resources to work with, the intel was gappy, and no one had the tools they needed to complete their various missions. *Adapt and overcome.*

Rumors had circulated among the troops even as the Mainers had boarded the plane for BIAP weeks prior that something weird had been going on at Abu Ghraib, but that was long before the photos were published abroad via television and the Internet. Until that happened, near the end of April, and even for quite a long while afterward, it seemed that the troops on the ground at Abu Ghraib knew less than anyone else on Earth about what was going on.

"What's going on, sir?"

"FUBAR."

The insurgents certainly seemed to be better informed. On March 20, 2004, the Department of Defense announced that eleven soldiers would be court-martialed on charges that they abused prisoners at Abu Ghraib. Almost immediately, mortar attacks, which had been a feature of daily life at Abu Ghraib from the beginning of its time as an American facility, became more frequent and more sustained.

Two all-out, mass casualty attacks occurred in April of '04, though it wasn't until April 28 that, after delaying broadcast for two weeks at the request of the White House, CBS showed the photographs of the abuse as part of a *Sixty Minutes II* report.

When Dizl eventually saw the photographs of Americans abusing detainees, he heard the cosmic screams of all the poor souls who had died in that hellhole: the thousands tortured and murdered by Saddam and then the dozens who had died before his eyes.

The Iraqis knew about it before the Americans did. It was, after all, their sons, brothers, fathers, grandfathers, and even sisters (there were women at Abu Ghraib, though not many) who were being kept in the prison. It was their relatives and friends who were the guards in the all-Iraqi part of the facility where only ordinary criminals were kept, or it was their neighbors who unloaded the supply convoys, collected the garbage, and emptied the porta-potties.

Among other evidence of disorder and neglect, the Taguba Report (the official US Army report of the investigation into the detainee abuses at Abu Ghraib) noted that three prisoners had actually escaped from Abu Ghraib during the same period in which the abuses took place, but even when information was not being carried out in the mouths of escapees, it remained perfectly possible to take advantage of the comings and goings of civilian workers and send and receive notes or messages. For that matter, it wasn't impossible in some parts of Ganci to wrap a note around a rock and chuck it over the wall, or for someone on the outside to pick it up, read it, and chuck an answer back.

Buildings taller than the walls that enclosed the facility surrounded Abu Ghraib prison. As is true in many of the world's hot, dry places, in Iraq a roof is considered living space and tends also to be easily accessible from the street. Anyone standing on the roof of a tall building could see right over the wall into Abu Ghraib. Or, if he were so inclined, he could shoot over that wall.

As the spring wore on, Graner's photographs appeared and were instantly weaponized, the insurgency intensified, and more and more people seemed to be shooting over the walls. Dizl knew it was going to be bad when he saw the photo of England with the prisoner on the end of a dog leash. *Oh, boy*, Dizl thought when he saw the photos. *Here we go.*

"This was a country where goats ride in the front passenger seat while the wife is in the back," Dizl said. "Women are not valued and there's an American woman leading an Iraqi man around on a dog leash." The photo of Specialist Sabrina Harman with an enthusiastic smile and a thumbs-up while leaning over a dead body said to the

Iraqi people, "American mothers, sisters, and daughters think dead Arabs are 'thumbs-up.'" Insurgents still show the pictures to this day. It's an understandably easy recruiting tool. "Guys that could have gone home on the happy bus got blown to flinders by mortars instead."

A mortar is a relatively simple weapon. It's easy to use as long-range, heavy weapons go, which explains its popularity among insurgent and terrorist groups. A modern mortar consists of a metal tube set at an angle to the ground, usually ranging somewhere between 45 and 85 degrees. As a rule of thumb, the higher the angle, the less distance the shell will travel. Gunners drop a purpose-designed bomb into the tube, where it hits a firing pin that detonates the propellant attached to the bomb's tail and launches the projectile.

There's no motor, just the mathematics of the arc. When the shell hits its peak, gravity takes over and the round falls to earth. The most modern shells come with assortments of GPS-driven steering fins and other high-tech bells and whistles. These are expensive and hard to use, however, and the insurgents did not have access to such technology. The most common shells used by insurgents are often the simple, mass-produced mortars with a fuse and detonator set in the nose that sets off the explosives inside. Those on the receiving end of these "low-tech" projectiles, however, would see little difference.

Well-trained mortar operators can drop shells on the enemy with impressive accuracy. Insurgent forces do not have the luxury of the level of training the allied forces have. Without a spotter, many of their rounds impact with little or no effect. However, when a spotter equipped with binoculars and a cell phone is positioned somewhere near the targeted area, he or she can dial the explosions in on one tempting target or another (hence the "walking").

Mortars, like other conventional weapons, come in a number of sizes and can carry various payloads. They can be filled with chemicals, both lethal and not. In fact, the Bad Guys habituating the area around the prison were constantly threatening to launch a sarin gas attack. Death by a nerve agent such as sarin is long and excruciatingly painful. The nerve endings in muscles lose the ability to shut off, resulting in horrific muscle contortions strong enough to break bones as the victim twists uncontrollably into inhuman shapes. Eventually the diaphragm ceases to function and the victim dies of asphyxiation, but only after suffering the bone-shattering, muscle-tearing effects of the gas.

Luckily, Dizl and the Mainers did not have to contend with a gas attack, as the insurgency had no access to it, but the standard high-explosive shells were doing enough damage by themselves. The HE inside a basic mortar is designed to fragment the metal casing into a thousand pieces ranging in size from a pea to a twisted ceiling fan blade.

The energy from the detonation expends itself outward, so the tail fin usually survives the blast and can be found afterward, sticking out of the dirt at the point of impact. Employing mathematical formulas bequeathed by Newton, survivors of the attack can use the angle at which the tail has thrust itself into the ground to determine the point of origin (referred to, mostly straight-faced, as the POO).

Assuming the mortar round behaves as advertised, the size of the resulting fragments won't matter so much as where they impact because the velocity behind them means they can apply a massive amount of force. A peppercorn shot through the head or into the liver can be sufficient to render a soldier "non-mission-capable" and/or dead.

Quality can vary when it comes to any product, particularly when the consumers are insurgents in an occupied country. Occasionally, the ordnance flung over the walls of the prison would fail to detonate. The duds would be carefully removed and taken to a safe open space where they would be detonated with another explosive.

This was a necessary measure but one that added yet more unnerving explosions to punctuate daily life at Abu Ghraib.

The radio crackled and Dizl heard Turtle asking for assistance with one of their regularly misbehaving Abu Ghraib residents whom the Americans called "Thumby." The bomb-maker had earned his moniker because when he decided he'd had enough of the insurgent lifestyle (so he said) and went to go get rid of explosives, they went off and he blew both his thumbs clean off.

Thumby appears in the annals of the Abu Ghraib scandal as the detainee who somehow managed to smuggle a gun into the Hard Site, and later for naming the bad apples of Tier 1-A who would become the subjects of the illicit photographs.

The gun Thumby got his hands on was smuggled to him by a guard who now resided as a detainee. The guard's "name" was ABB, or "Anal Bleeding Boy," thanks to his predisposition to inserting his toothbrush into his own anus. ABB fell in love with the Mainers and would toothbrush his ass while looking lustily into the eyes of passing rovers. While at first disconcerting, the Mainers eventually learned to roll their eyes at the amorous attention and continue about their fourteen-hour workday.

Graner and England were long gone, back to the States and courts-martial, but Thumby was still around, and he was a pain in the ass.

Thumby would do anything for a Marlboro, only really becoming crazy and dangerous when he was having a nicotine fit. Other detainees, once they learned this about their fellow prisoner, would pay him in cigarettes to hurl himself into the piles of razor wire.

"Thumby's cutting himself again," Turtle announced, somewhat unnecessarily, as the prisoner's arms were streaming blood when Dizl and Sugar showed up to help. Among the indispensable items not provided to the soldiers of the 152nd were adequate medical supplies. Dizl had trained as a combat lifesaver, but even he hadn't been issued a kit that would allow him to deal adequately with the daily minor injuries that come from working in a prison located in a war zone, let alone a catastrophic one. So he'd emailed his wife.

"Please send as many sanitary napkins as you can," Dizl wrote. "The kind with that long tail, if you can find them. Cram as many of those tampons as you can fit into a box. Make sure you get O.B. tampons because they're the right size to fit a bullet hole. Oh, and could you send some Ziploc bags, too?"

Once the package arrived, Dizl settled himself on the floor of the Mortar Café and made each of the guys in First Platoon a Ziploc bag filled with napkins and tampons, to be carried with them at all times.

So when Thumby was discovered in the isolation cage, his arms streaming blood from the cuts he had inflicted on himself with a piece of glass, the Mainers swathed his arms in Kotex—a clean, effective, "field-expedient" sanitary bandage.

NINE

APRIL

"American soldiers in Abu Ghraib were not injured Tuesday when guerrillas fired the barrage of mortar rounds into walls of the prison killing the 22 detainees, but 92 security detainees were injured—25 seriously."

—"Postcard from Abu Ghraib," Camden (Maine) *Herald*

THERE WERE ABOUT thirty MPs inside Ganci on April 6, 2004, the day things first got really pear-shaped and detainees started up one of their "Death to America" chants with fervor. From his tower, Dizl heard a voice on the Motorola radio pass along an order: "Use of force is to be set at the level of 'amber.'" This meant that a weapon could be loaded but there must be no round in the chamber.

A senior officer, smoking a cigar, wandered out to see what had the detainees all worked up so he could determine what orders to give if the rocks began to fly.

As the officer chewed on his cigar, Dizl loaded all his weapons to threat level red (for dead). Once his shotgun and pistol were ready,

Dizl loaded his M16. He had a pair of double-stacked thirty-round magazines fastened together with industrial-grade Velcro—a non-regulation piece of ordnance his brother had sent for just such an occasion. The major stood, damp cigar crammed in mouth, and watched him snap the double-stack into his weapon and pull back the charging handle. Dizl made sure the round had gone into the chamber before he tapped the forward assist and closed the ejector port cover, just as he had been taught to do in basic training at Fort Benning, Georgia, years before.

"Threat level is at amber," the major said.

"Yes, sir. I know."

Then Dizl aimed the M16 at a chanting detainee's head. If he had to shoot, he could only hope the bullet would pass through one head and hit a few more freaked out, homicidal detainees behind him. Dizl, like every other MP in Ganci, was facing down the common problem of too many potential hostiles and not nearly enough bullets. In that moment Dizl could've sworn he actually heard the major growl, like an angry dog, as he soaked up the reality of Camp Ganci.

Am I going to kill somebody? he thought. *Am I going to die?*

He didn't, not that day. But back home in Maine, a neighbor had taken to keeping a public count of the casualties of the Iraq war, representing each American soldier's death by a yellow flag stuck in his front lawn. They were a vivid memory for Dizl, the hundreds of yellow flags fluttering. He really didn't want one of those little flags flying for him.

The incident passed in seconds creeping slowly by.

One thousand one . . .

"One rock flies, I'm shooting you in the fucking face and blowing your head off."

One thousand two . . .

The detainees began noticing him and elbowing each other, nodding at the man pointing a gun at their collective heads.

One thousand three . . .

The crowd began to disperse, their complaints not enough to warrant facing down an armed man. They left an arch of stones marking where they'd been standing ready to riot only seconds before.

One thousand four . . .

End of incident.

At the start of Lunch Lady's shift on April 6, there was word from higher up that a mortar attack to cover a massive prison escape was planned for the day. Lunch Lady began his tower duties prepared to be vigilant.

He could never tell the difference between mortars and rockets, but he heard the first ones arrive and explode. He saw them "walking," just as Dizl had, and thought, *oh shit, they're coming right for me.*

A round tore through a detainee tent and smoke poured out of both sides. A single man walked out. He was missing a part of his foot. He looked at Lunch Lady, who saw the fear in the man's eyes just before he died and collapsed in a heap to the ground.

The lieutenant began yelling at the terrified detainees, and when one finally stopped screaming and looked, Lunch Lady pointed at the tent that had been hit. The detainee looked into the tent, puked and then staggered away.

The next guy who looked in gagged too, but did not leave. He waved urgently to Lunch Lady, imploring him for some kind of direction. The lieutenant pointed to a blanket that was draped across another tent, thinking they could use it as a stretcher. All but five men from that tent would survive the explosion.

"This heroic detainee went in and pulled a guy out," Lunch Lady later told his men. "He was still alive, though bleeding. As the wounded man was carried out, I pointed again to the blanket, and it was as if the hero could read my thoughts. He grabbed another guy who was running by, and they carried the wounded man to the aid station. The two of them came back over and over again. They carried all the detainees from that tent to the aid station."

The lieutenant, deafened by the explosions, hadn't heard the voices calling to him from the Motorolas, imploring him to answer and let them know he was all right. Skeletor arrived to the scene at last. Having seen the tower disappear amid a shower of explosions, he was certain Lunch Lady had been killed.

"Are you OK?" he shouted into his lieutenant's face.

"What?"

Skeletor shook his head and hugged him.

However, the chaos was far from over. Skeletor and Yogi managed to rescue most of the wounded from Ganci 4, though their efforts were delayed by some of the more fervent detainees in the compound.

"Stop throwing rocks!" Skeletor shouted through the wire. "Get down. You've got to get below the shrapnel." A rock flew past his head.

"Goddamn it," said Yogi. He lowered his shotgun and aimed it at the chest of the nearest rock-thrower. "Fucking shackers! We need you to bring us your wounded. Drop the *fucking rock*." Skeletor pointed his shotgun at them too. There was a brief, tense standoff, and then, to the Mainers' relief, the rock dropped to the ground, and the wounded started coming.

Those survivors with minor flesh wounds came to the gate under their own power, but others had massive, gaping holes and missing limbs and had to be carried. One man had his calf blown off and was bleeding profusely and screaming in pain. The guy Skeletor called Midget was brought up to the cage with a hole in his chest, already dead, no doubt killed instantly. Skeletor had time to remember seeing Midget go flying into the side of the shower point.

Then an old man with a long, grayish-white beard that was flecked with blood and shards of bone from his gaping chest wound took

Skeletor's attention. He was gasping for breath, his mouth opening and closing. He was pale and a pool of blood was growing fast in the dust beneath him. A man who went by Chiclets and the other medics were working on him, trying to stop the bleeding, but Skeletor could tell the old man was going to die by the way he looked at them.

The man who had had his calf blown off survived long enough to be loaded into the medevac, only to die on the way to Baghdad. The medics were able to keep dozens more alive long enough to see them safely into the hands of the doctors and survive the attack.

Coalition forces arrested Hussein abu Mastfa, along with a bunch of his relatives, for retaliating against a rival family. Hussein owned a trucking business and another family was trying to gain control of some of Hussein's territory. The families had an argument that turned violent and Hussein's niece was killed when his car was ambushed. Hussein, his sons, nephews, and cousins had been on their way to the rival family's home when coalition forces caught them. Hussein, imprisoned in Ganci 4 with his posse, quickly became the compound chief.

So after the first large attack in which detainees began chucking rocks at the guards, Staff Sergeant Hurtt, called—for reasons unknown—Tex, gathered Hussein and his relatives for a meeting. Through Firos, a detainee with a good enough grasp on the English language to be designated an interpreter, Tex told the detainee leadership, "I want you to know how sorry I am that this attack happened. I am sorry your friends and family members have been killed and injured. It was a horrible day for everyone, but I want you to know I am proud of how you reacted. The throwing of rocks was bad, but I understand that you were upset. Afterward, you helped us."

The tent chiefs listened, their faces grave. A few nodded agreement, or at least acknowledgement.

"If we should be attacked like this again, we will do our best to help save your wounded men, but you have to help us, too. No rock throwing, no rioting. Bring the wounded here, to the front, and we will help them. Thank you again for working with us. Together, we saved many lives."

As the deprivations of the siege continued to worsen, the prisoners of Ganci became quite unruly, all except the ones in Ganci 4. At one point, detainees in all the other compounds began hurling rocks at the towers, chanting, threatening to tear down their tents and fling them across the concertina wires, walk right out, and attack. Truth be told, they easily could have done this. The tent cloth was thick enough to have protected them from the sharp wire, and if several compounds tried it at once, the Americans would have been swiftly outnumbered and overrun. However, Hussein and his relatives rounded up the seven hundred or so detainees in Ganci 4. They made it clear they would not partake in the festivities; instead they all sat down facing away from the other compounds.

"I think they appreciated what Tex told them," Skeletor told Dizl afterward. "We may have earned a bit of respect from them." This change among the prisoners of Ganci 4 would continue; when the second mas-cas began, no rocks would meet the soldiers who arrived at the Shark Cage in Ganci 4.

Captain Morgan would remember thinking that April 20 was going to be one of the good days, because he would be sharing a tower with Dizl. He loved days like that, since solitude made a twelve-hour watch long. On the other hand, there had been intel about a possible attack. Sometimes a young warrior would hear intel about the Bad Guys getting frisky and look forward to a violent encounter. The men of the 152nd were at the point where the novelty of war had long since vanished.

It was another Groundhog Day for Dizl and Captain Morgan as the detainees were served their midday meal of beans and rice just before the changing of the watch at 1200. Following lunch, the detainees would endure Count and then they could do as they pleased until the evening meal, prayer, and bed. Captain Morgan was standing behind Dizl, performing an overwatch for some workers who were pumping out the detainee porta-potties positioned near the Hawk's Nest.

Because of the siege, the contents could not be trucked away, so they'd dug slit trenches to channel and contain the waste of thousands of people. The sheer quantity made it necessary to occasionally set the mess on fire, which was not a treat for those on duty in the Hawk's Nest, perched barely fifteen feet above the burning turds. Foul smoke wafted in from between the floorboards and made their eyes water.

On the plus side, Dizl thought gloomily, *the smoke might discourage the flies.*

He would've said it out loud to Lunch Lady but the flies were so thick that opening one's mouth risked munching a mouthful.

Someone was calling to Dizl.

"Shahein!" It was the boy, perhaps fifteen years old, who the Mainers had dubbed Young Elvis. He was calling Dizl by a nickname the detainees had given him. *Shahein* meant "Eagle," as Dizl must have appeared to them up in his tower, gazing down on the detainees with the intense focus of a great bird of prey.

"Shahein, there are bugs in the food," Young Elvis said. "No good, very bad, please help."

Dizl dismounted his tower—a no-no, but Lunch Lady remained to oversee the burning, so Dizl felt the area was sufficiently covered. A quick look at Young Elvis's white plastic picnic plate revealed what looked very much like little white worms or bug eggs. On closer examination, these proved to be the whitish sprout that sits in the indentation of a bean, but these had become separated from the beans during the cooking of the lunchtime stew.

A small crowd of detainees gathered as Dizl explained to Young Elvis that the white things in the food were not bugs but part of the bean. All agreed, through the wire, on the truth of this observation, but it was clear there would still be a problem when the stew was served to the thousands of detainees.

Standing there, in the stinking heat of Abu Ghraib, Dizl heard an echo from his old life in Maine. "Never make excuses for bad food," Marcel Lacasse Sr. insisted. Marcel was the French-Canadian chef at Marcel's Restaurant in Rockport, where Dizl had worked as a waiter years before. "If something is wrong, it may as well be your fault. Just fix the problem."

"Let me see what I can do," Dizl told the detainees.

The bean stew discussion between the detainees and Dizl took perhaps a minute. Dizl hustled back into his position in the tower and called Red, telling him to contact the chow hall immediately, and request more food.

"More food?" Red repeated, startled.

"Tell them that the problem really is bugs or they won't do it."

"There isn't enough time to get more food for so many people," Red protested.

"I've worked in large kitchens, Red. There's bound to be more of something, rice at least, because the detainees usually get rice twice a day anyway."

So Red made a call up the line. He called back: "More rice is on the way."

End of incident.

Total turnaround time for the new rice was, maybe, ten minutes. *Thanks, Marcel*, thought Dizl.

"Good man, Shahein," said Young Elvis.

And Young Elvis turned and ran back to his tent, which he shared with about twenty other detainees, two of whom were his brothers, known as Middle Elvis and Old Elvis.

Young Elvis wasn't the only child at Abu Ghraib. In fact, there were easily a dozen juveniles eighteen and under mixed into the horde prior to what Dizl called the "Great Sorting," after which those who had not been sent home were relegated to their own enclosure in Redemption, sited in Level Three so as to be closer to the watchful supervision and protection of the soldiers in the command post.

The Great Sorting was what the soldiers of the 152nd named the process of separating out and organizing detainees into different groups that would be easier to manage and hopefully, a little more harmonious. Through interviews and investigations, less threatening detainees were taken out from the more hardcore insurgents, and those likely to be innocent of anything but being in the wrong place at the wrong time started to get processed out of the prison and released. The idea was that common criminals, insurgents, and the innocent would be kept in different parts of the camp. Sunnis and Shiites would also be kept separate to help ease cultural and historical differences that could flair into violence.

At the time, there was no Iraqi equivalent of a Department of Human Services willing or able to take charge of juvenile offenders. Once the Great Sorting had taken place, the remaining children were, in fact, actual enemy combatants. Their skills ranged from expert IED manufacturing to being trigger boys and scouts for the enemy. These were kids to whom the Wahabis offered the carrot of cash and any number of truly scary sticks, which included the looming threat of a hole getting drilled in their skull.

When Marines at Fallujah or some other battle zone picked up kids, there was no place to send them other than Abu Ghraib.

Dizl considered that, given the alternatives, these kids were in good hands. They were being cared for by a bunch of dads, including him, and female MPs, many of whom couldn't help but think of themselves as surrogate moms.

The kids formed a group of little rascals, like the street urchins from *Oliver Twist*. As the kids taught him the Arabic names for beasts and birds, Dizl bestowed them with animal names in return. There was a sawed-off, rugged, grumpy, chain-smoking twelve-year-old he called Ah-neb (ant), while Tat-twah was named for a marsh bird that makes a *tat-tat* sound when alarmed. It seemed like an appropriate onomatopoeic name given that Tat-twah was always tattling on his buddies. There was a bird that looked a bit like a phoebe, an insectivore called a bulbul that hunted in the rolls of concertina wire for anything that skittered. Bulbul—the human—could creep through the wire and pick up bits of trash and treasure without getting snagged.

One day, the boys asked Dizl if he had a wife, and if she was *jameelah* (beautiful).

"Yes, I have a wife, and yes, she is jameelah."

They giggled and whistled and made curvy movements with their hands to indicate a shapely female body.

"*La! Madame pheel* (elephant)!"

"*Shanoo*?!" (wha-at?)

As he'd reached the limits of his Arabic, Dizl proceeded to stomp around like a mad she-elephant, waving his arm like a flailing trunk. The little monsters fell about laughing at him and chattering to each other. The idea that Shahein was married to a beautiful American woman the size of an angry elephant was an amusing one.

"She's the one who sent me to Abu Ghraib!" Dizl told them wryly, and they laughed and laughed.

Normally, by one o'clock, the detainees would be finishing their midday meal but, due to the bean stew incident, the lunch schedule had shifted a bit in Ganci Compound 7-1, so at least some of the detainees were still milling around in the open and hadn't yet returned to the shade of the tents to rest.

Captain Morgan was still performing his over-watch for the civilian workers burning the turds. The flies greeted Dizl's return to the tower with glad buzzing. From the tower, he watched the men finishing their food, scraping the last remnants of broth from their Styrofoam plates.

Young Elvis was smiling like a little leaguer who had hit his first home run and he gave Shahein a running thumbs-up as he passed the tower.

From the tower Dizl could see beyond the wall of the prison to where an Iraqi truck was towing a large agricultural trailer with a tarp over it. The truck crawled along the overpass that spanned the highway to Fallujah. The overpass hung in the air a few hundred meters from the western corner of FOBAG. The truck was moving too slowly.

For Dizl, time suddenly slowed to a crawl. The noise from the sewer pump was very loud. Young Elvis trotted toward his tent.

One thousand one . . .

Young Elvis, perhaps twenty-five yards from the tower, slowed to a walk.

One thousand two . . .

He was still giving Shahein a big thumbs-up, still smiling. The pump motor stopped, the flies buzzed.

One thousand three . . .

Young Elvis, like everyone else on the ground in Ganci, couldn't see the man perched atop the agricultural trailer training binoculars on the compound, but Dizl, reaching for his own binoculars, could see that the truck on the overpass had now almost stopped moving altogether.

One thousand four . . .

Young Elvis still smiled at the American in the tower. The spotter on the overpass was looking at the American in the tower too.

One thousand five . . .

Dizl turned his head, still reaching for his binoculars, picked up the Motorola instead, and screamed, "*Mortar!*"

When the first mortar struck inside Ganci 7 on April 20, Red was standing near the command post with Cowan and Bartlett. The force of the explosion flung all three soldiers over the vehicle. Red went flipping, head-over-heels, through the air over the length of the vehicle, landing on his neck behind the tailpipe.

I'm dead, he thought. An instructor's voice from years before popped into his head: *ten plus ten.*

He counted his fingers. He counted his toes. *All ten are there. OK, I'm not dead.*

Red sat up, his ears ringing and head stuffy. He saw Bartlett lying motionless nearby.

Bartlett is dead, he thought. *Where's Cowan?* But then Bartlett was on his feet and they were headed for the bunker tucked in beside the command post, when the next mortar—*krump*—flung them into the air again. Red picked himself up again. Bartlett was hanging in the camouflage netting.

OK, Red thought. *Bartlett is dead for sure this time.*

Bartlett began thrashing around, so Red helped him disentangle himself, then pushed him bodily into the bunker, which was very small and so dark it was impossible to see if anyone else was in there.

The concertina will have been breached. The detainees are going to be coming through the wire, he thought. *I have to secure the weapons in the command post or we'll really be fucked.*

"Stay here," he shouted to Bartlett. At least, it felt like he was shouting. He couldn't even hear himself and Bartlett just looked dazed. On his way out of the bunker, Red was blocked by something large and dark, and his hand was on his sidearm before he realized it was Cowan.

Together, he and Cowan secured the guns in the command post. They saw a mortar land close to Dizl's tower and explode. *Dizl's dead*, Red thought as the mortars continued falling as he unlocked the first gate in the Ganci 7 Shark Cage.

"Open this up," said an older man, one who had taken on the role of compound chief. He was standing before the second gate. "Let us bring the wounded men out of here."

"I can't," said Red. "I'm sorry. You'll have to bring them to the gate and let me take it from there. I can't let you out."

The compound chief shook his head angrily, and turned away.

Lunch Lady was supervising the sewage burning and the redistribution of food after the detainees thought they'd found worms when he heard the first mortar land. A dozen people still holding their lunch plates fell over like cut grass. Shrapnel and gravel flew outward at the speed of sound, blowing a man's legs clean off.

The body of a man, stretched prone with a gaping hole gushing blood from the middle of his torso, appeared in front of Dizl's tower where, a few seconds before, the smiling Young Elvis had been. Elvis was gone, disappeared into thin air as far as Lunch Lady could tell. The body hadn't been there when the shelling started; he'd been flown via Mortar Air from some other part of the compound.

Sergeant Bret King, a.k.a. Yager Bomb, came sprinting through the dust, blood, and chaos to fetch Dizl's rucksack that was full of their improvised medical gear. IV bags were all hooked up and ready to go with permanent marker instructions, and Maxi Pads, tampons for packing the meaty holes of the screaming wounded, and rolls of self-adhesive athletic-style bandage to hold the field-expedient first aid packing materials in place filled the bag.

Krump

Another mortar round landed, another deadly explosion splashed the inhabitants of Abu Ghraib with another wave of buzzing shrapnel. The three tents closest to Dizl looked as if a human meat cannon had been used to blast their occupants through the canvas ceilings. Ribbons of skin clinging to pieces of human meat fluttered down through the air in a grisly hail.

Dizl was alive but down, and he'd just watched Young Elvis die. The same explosion that killed the boy temporarily deafened Dizl and wreaked long-term, permanent damage to his brain.

"I saw him [Young Elvis] get blown to flinders," Dizl said, recounting the horrific event years later. "He was smiling at me, and giving me a running thumbs-up."

Still deaf from the concussive force of the rocket exploding, Dizl could only watch as sheets of the boy's skin flapped in the breeze from where they'd snagged on the razor wire, attracting clouds of carrion birds. Sparrows too, hundreds of European house sparrows, the ones that normally haunted the edges of Ganci perched on the wire, had swooped in to scarf up the lunchtime rice and other delicacies.

"Crows and ravens gobbled up the fleshy chunks of Young Elvis and the others before the rockets and mortars even stopped falling on us all," Dizl said.

Out of the muffled silence, someone called *"Coach! Coach!"* It was Roy, who had played forward for the soccer team Dizl coached back home in Maine. Roy was shouting in his face.

Captain Morgan stripped Dizl out of his body armor so he could check for shrapnel wounds. There was a wound above Dizl's collarbone. Morgan pulled out a splinter of metal and handed it to Dizl. It wasn't until later that Morgan noticed blood running down his own wrist; shrapnel had hit him too.

There were more explosions, but even if Morgan had been able to tell a mortar round from a rocket, or either from the sound of a VBIED ramming and detonating to breach the gate to the prison, all sounds were muted and indistinguishable now.

Dazed, Dizl got to his feet and tried to check his area. He could feel the onset of shock and (like Red) remembered his combat medic training. He loosened his clothing. He was getting increasingly dizzy, his head hurt terribly, and he had a sharp pain in his spine, just below the top of his body armor.

Krump

Meanwhile, Red was overseeing the triage near the Ganci 7 command post. The wounded leaned against the back wall of the building while the other MPs worked frantically to stop the bleeding, treat for shock, start IVs, stick in the morphine, and wrap the wounds protectively with Maxi Pads. One detainee wandered slowly all the way across the compound, blood streaming down his legs, and Yogi helped him through the gate. Red turned to find this man standing at his elbow looking up at him. The Iraqi held out his hand and it took Red a moment to realize the mangled, fleshy little package was the man's genitals.

"Help me," he said, in English.

"OK. It will be OK," said Red, though he knew it wouldn't be. "Go sit down right over there, buddy. I'll be with you as soon as I can."

Red watched as, obediently, the man walked over, slumped down against the wall, and died.

Looking down from the tower, Dizl saw Middle Elvis was screaming up at him, wide-eyed, his terror and anguish inaudible but obvious. His mouth was moving: *My brother! My brother!*

Young Elvis had been blown to flinders. His behind and hips had bounced off the tower; sheets of his skin still hung from the barbed wire and those useless old radio lines.

"*Shahein, where is my brother?*" Middle Elvis begged Dizl to answer him while the crows wolfed down the bits of what, less than five minutes before, had been a bright-eyed boy who loved soccer and the peanut butter crackers from the Mainer's MREs. And Middle Elvis's brother.

A crow flew past Dizl's face, with parts of someone in its beak, and he thought, *The crows have come and carried your brother away.*

Then, it was quiet, just for a moment, before the screaming began. Dizl heard (and still hears to this day) the petrified voices begging and screaming for help while the crows and ravens feasted. They, the crows and ravens, seemed very thankful and unafraid as they ate the fiddly-bits of people; the parts we all take for granted while we are still alive.

The shooting was mostly done. Middle Elvis was wandering around the compound in a daze, crying. At intervals, Dizl would hear his mosquito voice saying: "Please. Please."

When the all-clear sounded, several soldiers were sent into the enclosures to pick up what remained. The smoke dissipated while Dizl and the other soldiers attended to the wounded, evacuating those in need of urgent surgical care. They had to assemble the body parts that had been scattered about like grisly children's toys and match them to corpses before they could bury the dead in graves aligned with Mecca. Even when those gruesome tasks were over, generals still needed their paperwork.

"Sir, this detainee is believed to have been killed, by insurgent indirect fire."

"Believed to have been killed? What does that mean? Who believes this?"

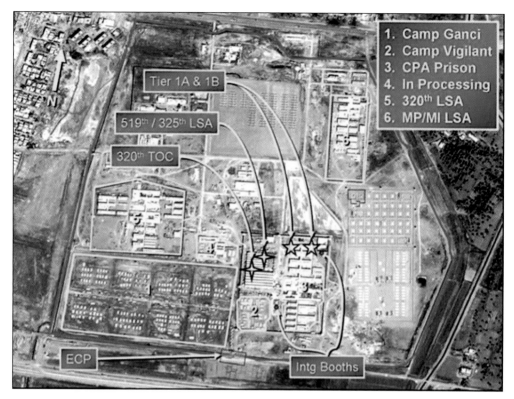

An overview of the Abu Ghraib prison the Mainers inherited.

The whole place was covered in trash and human feces. The soldiers were surrounded by the worst elements of human existence: pain, fear, hate, and garbage, endless garbage.

Detainees conduct their morning prayers.

Guard towers were cobbled together out of shipping containers and ingenuity.

Much of Ganci was located on top of an old landfill. Detainees could dig down through the dirt floors of their tents and find all manner of garbage that could be used to make weapons and even a radio.

One of many impact craters from insurgent indirect fire (a rocket or mortar).

This empty warehouse space would serve as the combat support hospital during the mass casualty events.

An old cell door in the courtyard became known as the Door to Hell. "If anywhere had the entrance to hell," Kelly Thorndike said, "it was Abu Ghraib."

Nearly every wall was decorated with smatterings of bullet and shrapnel craters, testament to what the Mainers and detainees alike endured.

Abu Ghraib was also home to stray cats. The Mainers adopted one of these and named it Hajji-Pussy. After Dizl saw that some of the KBR truckers had eaten a different cat, they made Hajji-Pussy a little collar that said "Please don't eat."

The Mainers hunted the plethora of rats that cohabited Abu Ghraib, competing to get the largest.

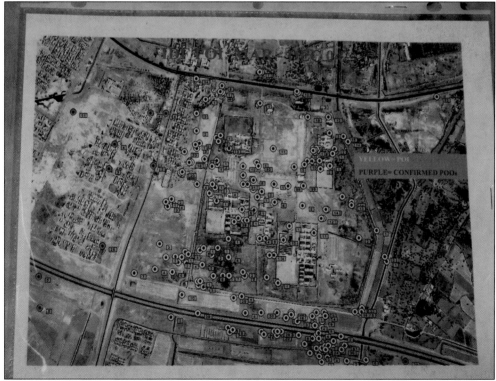

The yellow dots are confirmed points of impact, or where indirect fire like mortars and rockets landed and exploded. The purple dots are confirmed points of origin, or where the round was fired from. In the time it took the soldiers to figure out where the round had orginated from, the insurgents would have blended back into the civilian population.

Supply trucks that the 152nd brought with them to Iraq didn't have sufficient armor. So, the Mainers "up-armored" their vehicles with steel plates acquired from Abu Ghraib. These "homemade" armored vehicles were not unique to Abu Ghraib. Units all over Iraq were ill equipped with unarmored or too lightly armored vehicles.

2004/04/10

KBR fuel trucks burn after getting hit by an insurgent ambush. Resupplying Abu Ghraib became more and more difficult as the insurgency focused on the prison camp as the photos of the abuses there circulated the world stage.

A CH-47 Chinook helicopter lands carrying Secretary of Defense Donald Rumsfeld for his visit to Abu Ghraib.

Kelly "Dizl" Thorndike passes time during a moment of relative calm. Relaxation was almost impossible for the soldiers of the 152nd as mortars and rockets were nearly everyday occurrences.

Dizl and other soldiers from the 152nd at Fort Dix in New Jersey before they stepped off to the Middle East. Temperatures were in the single digits and they had no radios for the training event. Turns out, they wouldn't have them for their deployment either.

Dizl and some of the other Lost Boys snap a photo in Kuwait just before stepping off to head to Iraq, where they would spend the next year at Abu Graib prison.

"Oh, I believe it, sir. I saw him get blown to flinders, and the crows ate him before the mortars even stopped falling."

The dead needed to be identified and accounted for, the idea being that someone might be able to find out what had happened to their husband, brother, son, or uncle who'd been taken to Abu Ghraib, never to return.

The uninjured detainees were combing their compounds for the last bits, hoping to do their Muslim comrades the courtesy of getting whatever remained of them decently buried before darkness fell.

A sheet of skin still hung from the silent radio wires outside Ganci 7-1. Dizl had resumed his position in the tower after being treated by the medics. To his bruised and aching brain, the skin resembled an old-fashioned pocket handkerchief hung there to be bleached and cleaned by sanitizing rays of the sun. As he watched, the skin dried and shrank in the desert air. Eventually, it was a small, stiff, brown stick. A detainee paused next to the wire and gazed at what hung from it. Glancing up, he spotted Dizl. Raising his eyebrows interrogatively, the man cocked his head to one side and plucked at the skin of his arm.

Dizl nodded. "Yes," he said. "It's skin."

The man reached up, snapped the wizened brown stick from the wire, dug a hole in the dust with his toe, and buried it. The sun went down.

It turned out that extra sandbags Dizl had recently added to his tower saved his life by absorbing some of the shrapnel from the mortar that exploded nearby and deflecting the rest upward. The shards of metal dug themselves into the ceiling of the tower room, rather than into Dizl's face (Parker would amuse himself on subsequent watches by working pieces of shrapnel out of the plywood, to be saved as souvenirs).

On the night after the attack or, more accurately, in the wee hours of the twenty-first, when Dizl finally got undressed for bed, he discovered that his pockets, his underwear, and even his socks inside his tightly laced boots were full of sand. The mortar explosion had created a vacuum powerful enough to suck the sand from the damaged sandbags out of the air and blow it violently into the innermost recesses of his clothing.

The first reports of the attack filtering back to Maine National Guard Headquarters at Camp Keys in Augusta, Maine, claimed (inaccurately) that 90 out of the 120 Mainers had been killed that day. Investigators would later determine that at least forty mortars landed and detonated within the walls of Abu Ghraib prison, leaving twenty-two detainees dead and over ninety wounded.

Somewhere in Iraq, a mother mourns for her youngest boy, and a widow mourns for a husband. She does not know that he died flying, his transected head opening and closing like a child's toy, while a forty-year-old father of four from Maine covered the bodies of his comrades with his own, closed his eyes, gritted his teeth, and waited for death.

TEN

EATING BEES

"Lt. Gen. Ricardo S. Sanchez . . . issued orders that tactics like depriving prisoners of sleep, hooding them for long periods of time or forcing them into 'stress positions' to weaken their resistance to interrogation would no longer be allowed."

—*The New York Times*, May 14, 2004

I F AIR FORCE colonel Nelson had evaluated the situation at Abu Ghraib at the end of April 2004, he could have described it as, if anything, even worse than it had been during the deployment of the 800th MPs. Human beings do, simply, get burned out by relentless stress and suffering. April 29 was Sergeant Major Vacho's birthday. He'd just been given a cake when someone arrived with the grievous news that a soldier from another unit had put the muzzle of his sidearm into his own mouth and pulled the trigger.

Abu Ghraib continued to be "a troublesome arena even for a well-trained MP or MI (Military Intelligence) unit," and the former field artillery guys now designated MPs (Dizl insisted on calling himself a FAMP) were still lacking formal training, though the on-the-job education had been vivid and relentless.

The war continued with no end in sight, and the detainees would remain in fixed and exposed camp facilities, at least until the soldiers of the Sixteenth could build them newer and safer dwelling places.

Meanwhile, the photographs proved such a potent recruiting tool that the ranks of the insurgency began to fill with foreign fighters, many of whom only decided to join the insurgency after the infamous photos hit the world stage. Ahmad al-Shayea, a Saudi citizen who traveled to Iraq to join the insurgency and later went on to speak out publicly against al-Qaeda, was one such person called to action by the Abu Ghraib photos:

> Ahmad had to find the strength. He called the pictures of Abu Ghraib to mind. One of the Iraqis had said the hellish prison was not that far from them. He thought of all the young men like himself being held there, raped and beaten by the American Crusaders. He felt their pain in the pit of his stomach, his head pondering as if he too was hanging by his neck at Abu Ghraib. The jihadi told him the American Crusaders and Jews would not rest until they had killed every last Muslim.[9]

Abu Ghraib had been a previously neglected sideshow of Operation Iraqi Freedom. But it had now gained the attention of the international press as well as the United States government. In the aftermath of the revelations of prisoner abuse, the prison would receive a parade of visitors, including the secretary of defense, the secretary of the army, General Myers (then chairman of the Joint Chiefs of Staff), Lieutenant-General Sanchez, General Ryder (then Provost Marshal for Iraq), Major General Miller, and delegations from the International Red Cross and Amnesty International.

---

9 Ken Ballen, *Terrorists in Love* (New York: Free Press, 2012).

These people would be accompanied by any number of other foreign and Iraqi dignitaries, reporters, photographers, and television crews. Everything the Sixteenth MP Battalion did or neglected to do was being scrutinized through the magnifying lens of the scandal.

In sharp contrast to his predecessor, Brigadier General Janis Karpinski, who had no experience in detainee operations, Colonel David E. Quantock was full-time Army and held a degree in criminal justice. He had the right qualifications, and a serious, long-standing commitment to doing detainee operations properly.

One of the first things Quantock did was to clarify the role of military police at Abu Ghraib. Their sole task, for which everyone would be held strictly accountable, would be to provide safe and humane care to detainees. Again and again he repeated his message to anyone who asked (and quite a few who didn't). His troops would provide for the care and control of detained persons while treating them with dignity and respect. Period. He backed up the rhetoric with effective leadership. He showed up, got his hands dirty, and made sure his men were taken care of.

"I would eat bees for that man," Dizl said about Colonel Quantock.

Much, however, could not change. Quantock undoubtedly knew all about what a detainee facility should be like, but his troops, including much of the command staff, were still learning on the fly. Abu Ghraib remained at the mercy of its wartime geography, sandwiched between the hot zones of Baghdad and Fallujah.

In addition to missiles aimed deliberately at FOBAG, the inhabitants could easily become the collateral damage of nearby and unrelated firefights. For example, when a convoy on the highway was attacked, the soldiers in the convoy would return fire, and stray bullets from both sides would drop into the prison to ricochet off the concrete walls or go punching through an overflowing porta-potty. Plywood doors, the steel wall of a conex box, or the molded plastic side of a porta-potty provided no protection from flying projectiles.

Nearly every surface bore decorative holes or chunks missing from concrete walls.

Meanwhile, until the Great Sorting was complete, detainees remained a mixed bag (young, innocent, terrorists, criminals) stuck with deplorable, dangerous living conditions, and they remained frustrated and hostile.

When the smoke had cleared, and the explosion that could have killed him hadn't, Dizl's memories and longings for the sweet, calm life he had lived in Maine with those he loved slid down a hole inside of him to be locked away in some safer place and wait for better days.

I am here, still alive at Abu Ghraib, he thought. *What next?*

Piss in the corners, Dizl advised himself after a few minutes of self-reflection.

Pissing in the corners is a colloquial term among prison guards. It means getting in with the prisoners, getting into things, sticking your nose (tactfully) into other people's business, solving some problems, and creating a few for those who find themselves straying off a healthy path.

"It's like being a waiter in a fine restaurant," Dizl told Turtle with an expansive gesture.

Turtle looked dubiously at the tents, sagging dispiritedly from their tent poles, and at the trash.

"Seriously. A good waiter must be aware of every nook and cranny within his area of responsibility, and so must we."

That a guard at Abu Ghraib could be likened to a waiter at Marcel's would have seemed more unlikely, Turtle considered, except that it was precisely this experience that had allowed Dizl to manage the worms-in-the-beans incident.

"Roger that," said Turtle.

From the Hawk's Nest, Dizl had witnessed more than a few unpleasant *Lord Of The Flies*-style dramas among the detainees, and fellow guards reported similar incidents from their respective posts.

What to do? *Improvise, adapt, and overcome,* the age-old rule instructed. To this, Dizl added an adage gleaned from doing "custody and control" for the imprisoned citizens of Maine: *Piss in the corners.*

However, a Ganci tower guard, who saw all, was mandated to remain in the tower twelve hours a day, merely communicating—often without radios—all his observations to the mobile rovers on the ground, soldiers assigned to roam around the camp looking for trouble. Given that each enclosure held five to seven hundred detainees, with perhaps six or seven untrained MPs watching over them, there was no way to adequately police what happened inside the wire.

Perhaps it amounted to a Hail Mary pass, but Dizl had the sudden idea that if someone on the detainee side of the wire could be made to feel responsible for what was, in effect, public safety, the Americans might have a better shot at protecting everyone on the inside from the downright diabolical dangers intensifying on the other side of the wall.

So Dizl called for one of the rovers to cover his tower while Dizl went to summon Kathib, the self-appointed detainee czar of Ganci 7-1, who'd been running the place like a mobster and brazenly held court in a rat's nest of a tent right in front of Dizl's tower.

"Listen," Dizl said, when Kathib, with lordly reluctance, appeared on the other side of the fence. Echoing Tex, Dizl outlined some of his thoughts about the risks that detainees and soldiers alike were facing there at Abu Ghraib, and about how the dangerous choices of some of Kathib's people in Ganci 7-1 only put everyone in more danger.

"They are not my people!" Kathib protested.

"They are now," said Dizl. "You must keep things on your side of the fence as peaceful and orderly as possible, given the circumstances."

"*Asweech!* You are crazy!"

"Some say."

"This is impossible!"

"You must do it," said Dizl.

Back in his tower, Dizl didn't entertain any illusions about the conversation he had just had with the Iraqi. Doubtless for Kathib, abusive master of all he surveyed within the wire, the sentiments of the American on the outside sounded like the speeches of adults in old *Peanuts* cartoons. Dizl's humanitarian efforts were reduced to a few puffs on a wonky trombone. Still, it was a start.

"I'm hoping to make Kathib into what, in corrections terms, is known as a *change agent*," Dizl admitted, when Turtle asked.

As it turned out later, Kathib persisted in being the wrong guy for the job.

Soon after letting Kathib know that he would be held personally responsible for what did or didn't happen in the compound between the hours of noon and midnight, Dizl found himself in conversation with the Imam of the Ganci 7.

"I am not prepared to go through Kathib to get things done anymore," Dizl told him. "If there are things the detainees need, or if I see something go wrong, and I want a person brought to the wire below my tower, this must happen, with or without Kathib," he said.

"Yes," the Imam agreed.

"And I will treat bullies, liars, and thieves appropriately," Dizl continued. "This must be understood."

"I understand," the Imam said.

In the parlance of American prison culture, Kathib was "getting punked," served notice that he wasn't going be in control anymore. In fact, the thuggish Kathib was now Number One on Dizl's watch list.

In elucidating the new regime for the assembled detainees, Dizl made a gesture, a visual analogy of a hawk grabbing a rat, as he navigated the language barrier between himself and the Iraqis.

The interpreter turned to his followers and said, "Ah, Shahein!"

"Shahein," Dizl repeated. "Ayuh, that's me, and Kathib is *far* (the rat)!"

After that, whenever Dizl spotted Kathib or one of his minions punching another detainee, stealing food or clothing, or engaging in any other bullying behavior, Dizl would give forth an osprey's whistle and the detainees would respond by yelling, "Ahhhhhhhhh! Shahein!"

Being a businessman rather than an ideologue, the Ganci 4 compound chief, Hussein, was more willing than Kathib to make a pragmatic peace with the foreigners. As time went on, the relationship between the Mainers and the family group they called "Hussein's Mafia" became one of mutual benefit. If other detainees were fighting, stealing, or breaking compound rules, Hussein's relatives would turn in the perps and be rewarded with cigarettes, candy, and extra rations of food, which Hussein could then translate into even more peace and quiet.

The detainees were products of a far more authoritarian culture than the Mainers were used to, where dominance and force were expected and negotiation the resort of the weak. Compound leaders, like Kathib and Hussein, either commanded complete authority (whether by savvy or by fear), or they had none whatsoever. There seemed to be nothing in between.

The detainees were also, perforce, getting a sense of the Americans' way of doing things. Most detainees arrived discouraged, fearful, and defeated. In time, they would generally respond to the food, shelter, clothing, protection, medical care, and (eventually) family visits with at least some measure of cooperation and even gratitude. But others—the foreign fighters most notably—seemed to prefer thinking of this dignified and respectful care as a sign that the Americans had somehow been bent to the jihadists' will.

Removing a problem detainee from a crowded Ganci compound could take several days, because the best time to lay hands on them would be at Count. This took place three times per shift, though before the arrival of the 152nd, detainees were occasionally asked to perform the Count themselves. Unsurprisingly, the correct number would consistently be reported, though both malingering and escapes were common.

When it was Dizl's turn to supervise Count, he would have a team leader remove the difficult person from the line. Then he would summon the Imam.

The Imam, with evident disgust, would ask Dizl what should be done with this man.

"Ask him what his mother would say about his actions?"

The Imam would do so, and the detainee would hang his head.

"Now ask him what he needs? Is he hungry? Does he need a new prayer rug?"

An Imam had his own power among the detainees. The disgust on his face and the virtuous, Gandalf-like power in his eyes would sear the soul of any believing Muslim. This approach was far more effective than removing and isolating the troublesome detainee, and the public spectacle extended the reach of the lesson throughout Ganci.

So the detainee, who was generally squatting on the ground, would be required to stand up and admit to his misbehavior. He would have to apologize to the Imam for the aggravation he had caused, while Dizl added corroborative details of time and place from his notes and occasionally sketches he had made of the action.

Dizl would appeal to their humanity instead of their animalistic fear. Why back an animal into a corner with violence to get it to change behavior when food and respect work better?

How did Dizl have the fortitude to take care of men who might have just killed his brothers-in-arms? According to him, his duty had nothing to do with their crimes. Dizl had worked in the Maine state prison guarding guys who had "raped kids to death." It's a job, it's a discipline: create an environment of balance. It doesn't take a lot of people to do so, just the right ones.

The Mainers began figuring out the system that they'd inherited: their infrastructure. An infrastructure where, in the past, detainees would be mere feet away from a water storage tank and the plumbing wouldn't work. Before the Mainers, it seemed few units cared too much about following the basic humanistic procedures for taking care of prisoners of war.

So the soldiers found sustainable methods for detainees to have access to water, power, shelter, etc. The prisoners didn't have to get treated special; they just needed to see that the Americans would try to give them livable conditions, that the Americans were willing to move away from the bad habits of their predecessors.

"We transcended miles of fence with a little humanity," Dizl said.

He didn't put them there; his duties were limited to taking care of the detainees.

Slowly, over time, a balance could be detected, a fragile but definite sense of order based on more than the power of the guards' guns or the fear of the detainees.

As Skeletor intuited, the seeds might even have been sown during the terrible mass casualty attacks in April. After all those weeks of anxious anticipation, the blow had fallen, hard. It was a test.

By summer, there would be redemption. The April attacks got the attention of the generals and politicians and accelerated their plans for the new camp. It would have all the things that Ganci didn't have: bandages, hammers, radios, and the other necessary tools for running a prison.

There would also be surgeons, shrinks, dentists, even a pediatrician the local families could bring their children to see. There would be preventive care, like vaccines and bomb shelters.

There would be a combat library and movies for the detainees, even air conditioning for their tents, which was nice, since the average daytime temperature hovered around 130 degrees Fahrenheit.

In the desert heat, anyone with any sense spent the hottest part of the day seeking shade. To this end, for example, the hand-sized desert palm spider had developed the unnerving habit of dashing toward anything that might cast a shadow, including an American soldier.

Stripping off one's clothing presented itself as an obvious response to the intense heat. It was only with difficulty that the leadership could convince the men, especially the younger guys, to keep at least their underpants on when off-duty. There was a kid from Warren, Maine, whose dad had driven the school bus Dizl used to take to high school. He earned the moniker Roy-Roy-the-Naked-Boy because of his enthusiasm for nudity. The problem wasn't solely aesthetic; it was a matter of keeping vulnerable parts out of harm's way as much as possible.

Early in their deployment, a sniper bullet had buzzed past Huladog's head as he passed the fuel point one night, whanging off the structure of a diesel tanker before tumbling off into the darkness, an excellent case in point for anyone still unconvinced that it was prudent to remain "armored up" at all times. Boots, body armor, and a helmet became mandatory for travel between the Mortar Café and the porta-potties. The inevitable result was that exhausted men, or men with small bladders, would pee in empty water bottles to be disposed of later. Tolerances of this practice varied from person to person, and quarrels about the number and age of these bottles and what was considered acceptable provided Abu Ghraib's tenants with another diversion.

In the heat of the day, if you wanted to pick up or work with equipment that had been lying in the sun, it was advisable to wear gloves. Serious burns could result from something as simple as grabbing a hammer.

Incidentally, there would not be air conditioning for the troops' living quarters. This engendered resentment in the ranks, naturally enough, as even a Texan would find the climate a challenge, and for Mainers accustomed to fresh, cool summers, the hot nights were a misery from which one woke feeling halfway mummified.

"But it's a dry heat, isn't it?" folks back home would invariably ask, and Dizl would sigh patiently and say, "Yes, Iraq is a desert. It's a very dry heat."

One day around the middle of May, Dizl had been tasked with gathering a work detail of young detainees. They'd been shipped new tents, ones adapted for the promised air conditioning, and the detainees would serve as labor along with Dizl and other soldiers. The Iraqi sun burned down on them as Dizl traveled across the now-familiar gritty ground, moving from guard tower to guard tower, seeking shade just like a spider.

Pausing to catch his breath, Dizl found himself sharing the shade of a tower with a dozen or so small brown sparrows. They were perched on a bit of wire at about eye-level. Dizl had watched a lot of birds during his forty years, but he had never seen birds actually pant before. Nor did they move when Dizl appeared, let alone fly away. Instead, they just looked at him, stunned into apathy by the relentless heat, beaks open, heaving breasts working the air in and out of their tiny avian lungs. Dizl could have picked them like apples.

A couple of hours later, Dizl and his work detail were panting, too, with the effort of hoisting a new tent upright. Dizl knocked the last tent peg into the sand and wiped his hands on his pant legs, leaving streaks that would rapidly dry back into dust and salt. Glancing idly to the right, along the lane that ran between adjacent enclosures, he was startled to see a man with a machine gun. The man was clad incongruously in a dark suit, mirror shades, and a necktie.

Secret squirrel, thought Dizl—a term for the various CIA, DoD, or other intelligence contractors—whereupon, by way of confirmation, Secretary of State Donald Rumsfeld stepped into view beside his bodyguard. The fierce sun glinted off the Secretary's spectacles as he turned his head and looked down the lane toward Dizl and the Iraqi boys.

"Shit!" Dizl breathed.

The Iraqi boys looked at him enquiringly.

"Shahein?"

"*Yalla shabob*," Dizl hissed. He pointed urgently at the tent they had just erected. "Yalla SHABOB! Get into the tent!"

The boys dove for cover, with Dizl right behind.

"What is it, Shahein?"

"Shhh! *Lateesh*! No talking!" Their brown eyes wide, they leaned toward him as he put his finger to his lips and widened his own pale eyes to emphasize the seriousness of the situation.

"Rumsfeld!" he hissed.

"Rumsfeld!" the boys looked at each other, eyebrows arced, mouthing the word, grinning their astonishment. "Rumsfeld?"

"*Mushkalat*! Trouble!" Dizl nodded portentously. With exaggerated stealth, he reached into the cargo pocket of his dusty fatigues and drew out a stash of Tootsie Pops kept handy for just such an emergency. So they sat there together, lollipops jammed between chapped lips, a forty-year-old private and ten young Iraqi detainees, huddled together beneath the canvas, hiding from Donald Rumsfeld.

ELEVEN

HUMINT

"At a tent camp used for detainees with medical conditions, prisoners ran out shouting. Some hobbled on crutches; one man waved his prosthetic leg overhead. 'Why? Why?' he shouted in Arabic. 'Nobody has told me why I am here.'"

—Associated Press, May 6, 2004

A COUPLE OF years after they'd returned home, Dizl received a phone call from Chiclets. He had had enough; he couldn't take the images of the dead Marines' faces in his head any more. Unlike Dizl, who chose not to look at the faces of his dead and wounded comrades so he wouldn't have to for the rest of his life, Chiclets had had no choice. His mission at FOBAG mandated that he get very personal with them, the dying Marines, like holding their shattered skulls in his hands as he desperately tried to keep their brains from falling out.

Dizl was on the next ferry to Rockland. Chiclets, his young wife, father-in-law, and Dizl all took a ride down to the Togas VA to find Chiclets the help he so desperately needed.

A few years after that, in July 2011, Dizl was leaving the hospital after a surgery on his foot when he heard someone shouting his name, "Kelly! Hey, Kelly!"

It was Chiclets, who was now working as a VA nurse in the primary-care wing alongside Dizl's own doctor.

"I asked my primary-care doctor if she knew what they had in a guy like him," Dizl said. "She said, 'Yes, we do!'"

In the summer of 2003, the Center for Army Lessons Learned (CALL) sent a team to Iraq to review intelligence-gathering efforts in Iraq. The team found a series of wide-ranging problems in using technology and in training and managing intelligence specialists. Younger officers and enlisted soldiers were unprepared for their assignments, "did not understand the targeting process," and possessed "very little to no analytical skills," the CALL team found. It said that there were sixty-nine "tactical human intelligence" (HUMINT) teams working in Iraq, and that they should have been producing at least 120 reports a day, but instead were delivering a total average of 30. Overall, it said, the teams lacked "guidance and focus." They were also overwhelmed, and at least fifteen more teams were needed.[10] In August 2003, Captain William Ponce, an officer in the Human Intelligence Effects Coordination Cell, sent out a memo to subordinate commands. "The gloves are coming off regarding these detainees," he told them. (Quantock told his guys to put the gloves back on.)

Captain Ponce stated that Colonel Steve Boltz, the second highest ranking military intelligence officer in Iraq, "has made it clear that we want these individuals broken"—intelligence jargon for getting someone to abandon his cover and relate the truth as he knows it.

"Casualties are mounting and we need to start gathering info to help protect our fellow soldiers from any further attacks," he wrote.

---

10 Ricks, *Fiasco*, 192.

Ponce ordered them to "Provide interrogations 'wish list' by 17 Aug 03."

"I spent several months in Afghanistan interrogating the Taliban and al-Qaeda," a soldier attached to the Third Armored Cavalry Regiment, operating in Western Iraq, responded just fourteen hours later, according to the time stamp on his email. "I firmly agree that the gloves need to come off." With clinical precision, he recommended permitting "open-handed facial slaps from a distance of no more than about two feet and back-handed blows to the midsection from a distance of about 18 inches . . . I also believe this should be a minimum baseline." He also reported that "fear of dogs and snakes appear to work nicely."[11]

Some of the guys from Maine—Humpty for one—had never been on an airplane before being told they were heading overseas. Humpty had never set foot outside the United States; he could count on one hand the number of times he had left the state of Maine. In fact, he seldom departed even Hancock County, in which he had been born and raised.

As much as television and films could prepare him for the appearance and customs of people outside of Downeast Maine, and as easy as it had been for Humpty to form friendships with the African American and Hispanic soldiers he would work with, nothing had really prepared him for the culture shock that was Iraq, especially in Abu Ghraib. Maine had only recently fallen from its spot as the whitest state in the United States to number four, so anyone with a little melanin in their skin appears quite foreign to kids growing up in rural Maine.

However, Humpty—as well as some of the men from the more cosmopolitan regions of Maine—was completely unprepared for the

---

11 Ricks, *Fiasco*, 197.

appearances, habits, and customs of Iraqis, and soldiers of the 152nd found them distinctly, sometimes unfathomably, exotic. Humpty never got used to the calls to prayer echoing from the spire of the local mosque, whose onion-domed tower was visible from almost everywhere in Abu Ghraib.

Dizl, on the other hand, liked the haunting, song-like calls, and the tidy rows of synchronized worshippers that would form within the wire walls in response to the song of prayer. He found the Iraqis themselves, with their liquid dark eyes and flashing smiles, aesthetically pleasing as a rule.

"Some of them are pretty unattractive, though," said Turtle, when this subject was broached one day in the Hawk's Nest. "Thumby, for example."

"Some of us are pretty ugly too," Sugar pointed out. "You, for example."

"Well, that's a point," Turtle conceded. "Though Alison says I have an air of distinction."

It is sometimes claimed that Iraq is an "artificial" state, whose borders, set by European powers in 1920–21, did not respect ethnic or tribal boundaries. It's true enough as far as it goes, but the same could be said of many nations (the United States and Canada, for example). The people of Iraq may not be as diverse as Americans, but any given Iraqi's DNA might sport the genes of the original Ubadians who settled along the fertile, muddy banks of the Tigris and Euphrates Rivers mixed in with the genes of immigrating or conquering Sumerians, Babylonians, Assyrians, Akkadians, Persians, Greeks, Parthians, Romans, Arabs, Mongols, Turks, Kurds, and maybe even a more recent sprinkling of Brits dating from the heyday of British Colonial rule.

So while dark hair, dark eyes, and a semi-permanent golden tan were common to most of the detainees (while their captors presented the usual glorious American confusion of traits and features), green eyes and even blond hair were not unknown.

There was an unusually pale Iraqi detainee, a redhead known as "New Hampshire" because, to the Mainers, he looked less Iraqi than Irish.

"How did you get here?" Sergeant Doug Horton asked New Hampshire one day.

"Oh, mister-mister! The army took me from my bed and sent me to Abu Ghraib!"

"No kidding?" the sergeant exclaimed. "The exact same thing happened to me!"

As it turned out, the United States was snatching Iraqis up faster than they were deploying troops to guard them. The ratio of prisoners to guards in January 2004 when the 152nd arrived was seventy-five to one. By the following September, the ratio was a far more reasonable ten to one.

Much of the overcrowding was unnecessary, as many of the occupants of the prison were there for no other reason than their age and geographical location when allied forces passed through on one mission or another. The overpopulation made it difficult to identify the real insurgents who would have actionable intelligence.

As the Abu Ghraib scandal played out in the United States during the spring and summer of 2004, military officers who had maintained a loyal discretion regarding the administration's most egregious errors were now moved to name this Charlie Foxtrot (clusterfuck) for what it was.

Army planners knew what problems the lack of a good wartime detention facility would cause and tried to warn of the potential pitfalls. However, they and their advice had been shut out of the post-war planning effort. They had been told instead to focus on defeating the Iraqi Army and toppling the Saddam Hussein regime.

"In many cases, the tension between military brass and Rumsfeld centers around efforts by the secretary's inner circle to shake up longstanding military practices and assume greater risks," reported the *Christian Science Monitor*. "This has included using smaller numbers of troops, streamlining what he sees as a slow, cumbersome military planning process, and also placing a high emphasis on gathering 'actionable intelligence.'"

It was the pressure to gain actionable intelligence that inspired Bush administration and senior military officers to authorize "enhanced interrogation techniques" (i.e., torture). But more to the point, it was this pressure that led soldiers and Marines in the field to pluck up any potential source of HUMINT they encountered and stuff them into the deplorable conditions of an already overcrowded prison. Presumably some of these sources proved helpful, but the remainder—the majority—were simply, miserably, and unjustly stuck.

At his direction, soldiers under Colonel Quantock's leadership stepped up the effort to distinguish and separate the innocent from the guilty, and those suspected of insurgency from those charged with ordinary crimes. The latter were transferred to the tender care of their countrymen when the Hard Site was turned over to Iraqi control in September. Female prisoners were put under the care and protection of female MPs in the Hard Site and were eventually freed. And, most heartening, detainees who had spent months behind the wire at Ganci began at last to get their day in court. Many began to go home.

"If you don't release people, you only end up creating more insurgents," now major general Quantock said. "Prisoners getting let go can be leveraged to calm the insurgency. Release became an integral part of our operation as opposed to an afterthought."

During this period, Quantock also let it be known that anyone brought into Abu Ghraib had to arrive together with documentary evidence of his crime to justify the detention and later to be used in a hearing or trial. The colonel would permit no more roundups of men of military age to swell the population of Ganci beyond its capacity.

There were those who complained bitterly about this policy, commanders in the field who resented being asked to gather evidence or articulate probable cause. In short, warriors were told to behave like policemen. They also feared, perhaps with some justification, that the detention system had developed a revolving door, and terrorists were being released to cause more harm to American troops and Iraqi civilians.

Counterinsurgency warfare, according to Quantock, however, places a higher premium on the opinions of the populace than on the safety of the troops. Every prisoner taken to Abu Ghraib had left an estimated minimum of twenty friends and relatives behind. If he was imprisoned unjustly, or treated badly, those who loved him would be infuriated, and everyone they expressed their feelings to would have further cause to resent, distrust, and even wish harm upon the Americans. Such resentment and distrust undermined what tentative interest Iraqi citizens might have had in cooperating with the American effort.

"Treat [detainees] with a little bit of dignity and you can work wonders," Quantock said.

To that extent, the commander pestered General Miller for more resources. Better food and gravel to get the prisoners out of the mud were but a few improvements. The detainees also began getting access to reading and math classes from local civilians contracted and vetted by the army. Moderate Imams would visit to talk jihadists down from their radical pedestals.

"I wanted them to join the team," Quantock said.

And join the team they did. Quantock said that the amount of information coming out of the camps increased many times over.

"It's hard to prove," he said. "But I know the changes saved countless lives."

So spirits were high when eight of the Ganci 4 compound chief Hussein's family had been cleared of their charges and were going to be sent home. They were moved to the area used to hold detainees pre-release. Yogi had bought a box of Cuban cigars on his most recent expedition to the Green Zone, and he asked Skeletor if he'd like to go down to the pre-release compound and have a cigar with Hussein's boys.

They brought the Husseins out of the compound and sat down with them on the makeshift cement-block-and-board benches. There were no handcuffs or shotguns; just some cold Pepsi, a box of Cuban cigars, and Firos, to translate.

"We all sat around and chilled with them, human to human, not soldier to prisoner," Skeletor later told Tex. "It was a really nice moment."

It was a way of thanking them for working with the 152nd, and not against them, during the terrible events of April.

"Good luck. Be well," the Americans and Iraqis told each other. Then the Iraqis boarded the bus home, and the Americans walked back to Ganci.

The release of an Iraqi prisoner from Abu Ghraib did not occur in the manner made classic by countless crime dramas on TV; they were not simply deposited outside the front gates. Rather, commanders determined that the most humane course would be to bring detainees back to the locale where they'd originally been arrested. The prison provided transportation by what became known as the "Happy Bus."

For some, it wasn't always quite so happy. The rules said that they had to be brought back and released where they were initially apprehended, and this didn't always sit well with the released detainees. This could cause problems if a former detainee was returned to a place where he wasn't especially welcome. Cultural lines and neighborhoods had been shifted and splintered by the war, meaning a Sunni neighborhood might have changed to Shiite over the course of a prisoner's stay with the Mainers.

After the photo scandal broke, and rumors of further abuses, including the rape of female prisoners, began circulating, women who had been imprisoned at Abu Ghraib returned home to find that they were judged damaged goods, whether or not they had in fact been raped.

And there were some, though not many, who rode the Happy Bus out of Abu Ghraib only to be brought back, having demonstrated their jihadist bona fides in some regrettable act of re-offense. This would be true, for example, of the detainee dubbed New Hampshire.

Though Sergeant Horton had nothing to do with New Hampshire's departure on the Happy Bus, he had been known to inquire on behalf of detainees whose protestations of innocence sounded particularly plausible.

Middle-sized, squarely built, with fierce eyebrows and a bristling mustache, Horton could easily be typecast as the tough-as-nails Gunny in a World War II movie. His courage under fire, which would be amply demonstrated on more than one occasion, was matched by an unsentimental, clear-eyed empathy for the detainees in his charge.

There were of a couple of men whose honesty seemed so evident to him, for example, that Horton was moved to make inquiries among the Secret Squirrels on their behalf. Pressed, the Secret Squirrels admitted they really didn't have much evidence that these guys had done anything wrong other than be present in the wrong place at the wrong time. With that assurance, Horton made an energetic case to the command staff that the hearing process be expedited, and the two were heard and released.

It turned out that the two men were not only ordinary, law-abiding citizens of Abu Ghraib, they had served on the local town council. "*Shukhran*, mister-mister, thank you. You are kind, *hanoon*," they would say to Horton before boarding the Happy Bus.

Nothing about New Hampshire suggested he possessed much in the way of civic virtue. Still, he was set loose.

"Haven't I seen you here before?" Horton asked, upon spotting a mop of carroty hair on the other side of the wire.

"No, mister-mister! Not me," said New Hampshire.

If Horton was inclined to doubt his own memory, the newly installed eye-scanning technology at the Secret Squirrel shop confirmed it: New Hampshire was a repeat offender. His crime-against the coalition? Placing an IED along a roadway.

One day, during one of his frequent across-the-wire conversations, Horton conducted a very informal poll of a group of a dozen or so of New Hampshire's fellows who had been detained on the same charge.

"Money?" he asked each in turn, and each in turn said yes, they had been paid for improvising or placing an explosive device. As Horton points out, this was no small matter in a country whose economy had been as thoroughly wrecked as badly as its infrastructure by the combined effects of decades of mismanagement, war, sanctions, more war, looting, corruption, and the abrupt dismissal of thirty thousand employees of one of Iraq's largest employers, the Iraqi Army.

If the money needed to feed one's family wasn't sufficient incentive, al-Zarqawi's jihadists offered an additional one: Work with us, or we'll take a Black and Decker and drill a hole in your head. They meant it, too. Horton's information was that the unusually unpleasant prison bully the Mainers had nicknamed Lucifer had been one of the head-drillers.

Lucifer was also one of the more troublesome detainees and fought guards most chances he got. This grew tiresome. It meant, for example, that every time he needed a shower, medical attention, or rescue from the lethal clutches of a fellow prisoner, someone had to physically overpower him.

One day, Yogi called the command post requesting assistance at the isolation cage, and Dizl went to see what he needed. The isolated detainee had expressed a need to go to the bathroom, Yogi explained, and would need an escort, but Yogi couldn't leave his post. Would Dizl take him?

"Sure," said Dizl. "Who is it?" He craned his neck for a look. "Oh, come on! Lucifer is in isolation again?"

"Yup," said Yogi.

"And has to go pee again?"

"That's what he says."

"Jeeeezus. For a terrorist, that guy has a tiny bladder!"

"I know. And he's going to fight you."

"I know," said Dizl ruefully. He sighed. "I'm tired of fighting Lucifer, Yogi," he said. "I'm an old man."

"You'd think, if he really needed to go to the bathroom, he wouldn't fight the guy who's helping him out."

Dizl brightened. "Maybe if we give him five or ten minutes, he'll have to go so badly, he'll be too focused on that to bother fighting me? And then, when he's done, he'll be so happy and relieved . . ."

"How badly do you think Lucifer would have to go before he's too distracted to fight?"

"I say it's worth a try," said Dizl.

As it turned out, Lucifer didn't cause too much trouble that day, but the next time Dizl had to deal with him, Lucifer's bodily needs must have been met more recently. He tried to karate kick Dizl in the throat. Lucifer lost the argument, but Dizl retained an injury to the ball of his right foot that would require repeated surgeries during ensuing years.

One of the numerous problems Dizl and the other Mainers faced was a lack of instruction; they had no real SOP. Dizl had never even laid eyes on an operations manual for Abu Ghraib Prison. This seemed very strange; every branch seems to have a never-ending supply of thick manuals covering everything from invading a country to the proper adornment of medals on a dress uniform and when you're allowed to wear what kind of hat. Asking around, however, he discovered that no one seemed to have come across anything so basic and useful as directions in prison operations.

In the side pocket of his fatigue pants, Dizl carried a fat little book entitled Soldier's Manual of Common Tasks (Skill Level One), Soldier Training Publication 21-1-SMCT. Its cover was thickly reinforced with olive-green duct tape and annotated with ballpoint pen. Dizl had written "NEVER SNIVEL" in bold lettering across the front. In this volume, there weren't any instructions for guarding a prison, let alone for guarding a prison that combined such a diversity of offender-types. There was no guidance on how to manage the care and control of, for example, children who also happened to be murderers, bomb-makers, and enemy combatants.

So, adapt and overcome. Dizl emailed his wife: "Could you send me my old Maine State Prison Policies and Procedures Manual?"

She did, and the Mainers reviewed this document carefully, adapting its provisions to the Iraqi reality. It worked surprisingly well. Later on, after they had survived the heaviest of the insurgent attacks and had begun to build Camp Redemption, a question arose as to what should be done with stubbornly violent detainees who refused to behave themselves.

They opened Dizl's Maine State Prison Policies and Procedures Manual and found a human solution, a painless means of attaching meaningful consequences to bad behavior: the restraint chair. The restraint chair was pretty much exactly what it sounded like. It had a similar appearance to an electric chair, though it came without the bits and pieces required to make it an execution tool. It was designed to keep an unruly prisoner secured via restraints on the arms, legs, and forehead in a manner that didn't cause any pain as long as the occupant didn't struggle too much.

Following the specifications given in the manual, Dizl and the Lost Boys commissioned the chair for Camp Redemption, installing it on a smooth concrete platform in a sheltered area. A Red Cross delegation that was touring Abu Ghraib at the time specifically signaled its approval of and even admiration for this response to inmate violence.

Colonel Quantock marveled publicly about the 152nd's remarkable versatility. "They can make just about anything happen," he said.

TWELVE

LENNY THE LOBSTER, HAJJI-PUSSY, AND FRANK

"[D]etaining the family members of anti-Coalition forces, destroying the homes of captured suspects . . . and shooting at Iraqi vehicles that attempt to pass Coalition vehicles . . . may bestow short-term tactical advantages. However, these advantages should be weighed against Iraqi sentiments and the long-term disadvantages associated with the image it creates."
—Study by the Center for Army Lessons Learned, *Fiasco*, p. 253

A S MAY DREW to a close, there was a note on the camp message board. It said, "Make mental note that ICOs [Iraqi Correction Officers] will be taking over the Hard Site today (040521). This means that you will see Iraqis in the area and in the towers around the Hard Site carrying AK-47s. Their uniform is not known at this time. *Do not shoot them!*"

"What's going on?"

"FUBAR."

Camp Bucca, a new compound built to help with detainee overflow, safely situated near Umm Qasr and the Kuwaiti border, needed more troops to reinforce the Sixteenth MP Brigade. So commanders took a platoon of Mainers away from the already understaffed mission at FOBAG.

There was also good news, Big Army announced cheerily. The Lost Boys who'd been living in the Mortar Café were being moved into trailers being constructed in an area known to soldiers and Marines as Mortar Field.

In other words, the higher-ups had decided to take an empty area rumored to be a mass grave, an area no detainee would go near, and turn it into a trailer park for all the personnel at Abu Ghraib. Doubtless the trailers themselves would have been downright luxurious compared with the minimal amenities offered by the Mortar Café. And if you're already dwelling within the dubious feng shui of a torture chamber, living atop a mass grave couldn't be a whole lot worse.

The problem with Mortar Field was, in a word, mortars. The area had been thus dubbed for a reason, and if anything could make a cement-block building twenty-five yards from a fuel point seem a haven of safety, it was the idea of living in a tin box on Mortar Field.

There was immediate resistance on the part of the troops—Dizl declared that he planned to fill his trailer entirely with sandbags, and live underneath it—but the really effective resistance came from Captain Trevino.

Naturally, his resistance did not take place at a time or manner observable by the troops. Trevino was (and remains) a tactful man and team player. Nonetheless, though few of his men at the time knew this, he risked his bars when he refused to move his troops into Mortar Field. KBR doubtless got paid for the trailers anyhow, but the Lost Boys never moved and many of them today attribute many saved lives to Trevino risking the future of his career.

Around the middle of May, accompanied by a crowd of reporters, Rumsfeld and General Richard Myers, chairman of the Joint Chiefs of Staff, arrived at Abu Ghraib to see firsthand the improvements being made at the prison. Before their tour began, both men spoke briefly to about a hundred soldiers gathered in the dining facility, or DFAC. The general thanked them for their service and sacrifice.

Rumsfeld's remarks focused mostly on the photos of prisoner abuses, by then widely broadcast and published.

"It doesn't represent America, it doesn't represent American values, it doesn't represent the values of each of you," Rumsfeld said. "America isn't perfect, but don't let anyone tell you that America's what's wrong with this world," he continued, adding, "It's not."

For reasons best known to himself, Rumsfeld did not take a look at Tier 1-A, nor any portion of the Hard Site, soon to be turned over to the Iraqis for use as a traditional correctional facility. The tour of Ganci was, more or less, a "windshield tour."

Colonel Quantock described for reporters and the secretary of defense some of the safety measures the prison staff had taken to ensure detainees' safety. Each tent was now surrounded by sandbags stacked three high on all sides, and each enclosure had at last been given concrete bunkers to protect detainees from mortar attacks.

Quantock explained that Redemption, the new camp still under construction but soon to be completed, would feature several improvements to make the detainees yet more comfortable. Camp Redemption would be covered in gravel, where Camp Ganci was all mud. Tents would have wooden floors, and prisoners would have cots to sleep on. Redemption would have electricity and, eventually, heating and air conditioning in the tents, Quantock told reporters.

"We're going to do a lot better with this one," he said of Camp Redemption.

It was a recurring theme for any official briefing the press about the prison to emphasize that Quantock and the Sixteenth MP Brigade had taken command of the prison well after the abuses took place. When asked, Colonel Quantock acknowledged he had "been told there were problems" when his unit was transitioning to Abu Ghraib in January of '04. He had assumed, or even hoped, that the list he received included all the hazards, miseries, and deprivations of the place.

"It's all about leadership standards," said the colonel in summary. "And that's what we've been focused on every day."

It might have been pride or homesickness that inspired the 152nd to raise the Maine flag above the Mortar Café, where it flew until the anxious command staff fell prey to the fear that local residents might see it as a gesture of conquest. The flag came down to be replaced briefly by a pair of Scooby-Doo boxer shorts and then by the durable Lenny.

Lenny was a full-sized boiled-scarlet plastic lobster, the kind sold in tourist shops all over Maine. With the admirable patience only a plastic crustacean could muster, Lenny endured hundreds of trips up the flagpole, his plastic claws threaded through the flag-lines, and long, shell-melting days in the sun. This was hard duty, but Lenny did get a break. Sometimes, when one of the men went home on leave, Lenny received a tiny set of handmade documents, including a passport, so that he, too, could get away from the 'Ghraib for ten days or so of refreshing Maine normality.

The soldiers of the 152nd worked an average of seventy-eight hours a week at Abu Ghraib, with frequent workweek extensions. The soldiers occupied in detention operations frequently found themselves working up to eighteen days in a row, totaling 234 hours without a day off.

With such a demanding work schedule, there was limited personal time. A thirteen-hour workday leaves a scant eleven hours in which to eat, sleep, call home, or recreate.

"A musician must make music, and an artist must paint, and a poet must write," Abraham Maslow said of the human need for self-actualization. And everyone likes a little fun now and then.

Dizl had a travel guitar, and he painstakingly decorated its smooth wood with precise, tattoo-like ink drawings of Ganci Tower

7-1, of bones and stones, of a lizard and the twining, ever-present barbed wire.

Though Turtle was not the only soldier at Abu Ghraib who wrote letters home, his dedication to the handwritten note was unusual. Email and Skype were available, at least intermittently, even to the lowliest private, and most communicated with their families and friends with phone calls and video chatting. However, Turtle seldom used either. Email, he declared, was insufficiently personal, not to mention prone to the risks of accidental deletion or distribution. Skyping was just too painful.

"Seeing her and hearing her makes it harder to accept being without her," he admitted.

The courtyard outside their LSA provided space for a volleyball net, though the presence of bones, broken glass, and used hypodermic syringes made a no-diving rule necessary, even after a few wheelbarrows of sand were hauled in.

"Lickies" and "chewies," the name detainees gave to the candy provided in care packages from home, provided a certain amount of entertainment once they began to arrive. In the early days, snacks, condiments (sugar, cinnamon, anything to vary the flavor of the food), batteries, and pornography were items of inestimable bargaining value. "For *some* of the guys," Dizl amends, presumably to put distance between him and the porn. The appearance of a bag of Skittles or some peanut butter crackers from a soldier's pocket could often turn an encounter or discussion with a prisoner into an amicable one.

Some of the Mainers persuaded a KBR contract interpreter to give them Arabic lessons, and they studied assiduously. When sent to Baghdad as an escort, Dizl purchased an Arabic-English dictionary and a couple of old tourist maps of Iraq from one of the peddlers who had set up shop inside the Green Zone. In addition to soaking up some of the countless tedious hours, it built communication that helped lay a foundation of trust.

Those with a genuine aptitude for creating Let's Put On a Show in the Old Barn–style entertainment managed to pull off karaoke nights at the DFAC, and a boxing night that was a huge hit with spectators and participants alike.

When a small weight room was added to the amenities of FOBAG, some of the guys began exercising, and tanning. While the tanning didn't have any additional fitness benefit, it presented itself as an attractive pastime to pasty Mainers seeking ways to preen, especially when a few days of R&R at home was in the foreseeable future. Readers combined exposure to the sun's relentless rays with exposure to fine literature, ranging from *Dune* to Kipling, *Hunting Dog* magazine to an increasingly shabby copy of *Penthouse*.

Once the detainees were settled into the newly built and elec-trified Camp Redemption, Sugar became the unofficial "Combat Librarian" for the detainees. He made a project out of gathering and offering Arabic books and dubbed DVDs to the guys under his responsibility. The Pixar film *Finding Nemo* had to be yanked from circulation when the Ganci Imam told Sugar, "It is satanic."

This story of a father fish in search of his missing fish son became a favorite among the Lost Boys of the Mortar Café. As it happened, there was a real-life father-son pair serving together in the 152nd at Abu Ghraib. The father ran the motor pool and thus was known as Jiffy-Lube, while his boy became Lube Junior.

In June, both father and son flew home on leave for the occasion of Jiffy-Lube's stateside wedding and—more impor-tantly from the point of view of the Lost Boys—the accompa-nying bachelor party. Sharing descriptions of sexual interludes is time-honored entertainment for heterosexual men forced to dwell, womanless, together for long periods of time with nothing to do. By the time the father-son team departed for the United States, the material available in the collective memories of the men of the 152nd had been mined so assiduously, the tailings recycled so often by telling and retelling that the sources had really been exhausted. The return of the newly married (and newly step-mothered) Jiffy-Lube and Lube Junior represented a chance to hear some decent new tales.

Naturally, the subject matter would not be drawn from the wedding night. Wives, like mothers, are sacrosanct. Rather, they would hear tales from whatever excitements had been added to alcohol to make Jiffy-Lube's last moments of unmarried life memorable and interesting to the eagerly awaiting men back in Iraq.

When Lube Junior appeared at the Mortar Café, the first question, which Dizl claims Beerboy asked, while Beerboy indignantly pointed the finger at Night Rider, was "were there girls? Strippers?"

"There was one . . ." Lube Junior admitted. He was a round-faced, lamentably inexperienced young man, one forced to remain a perpetual listener during the after-hours storytelling sessions. Here, thought Night Rider, was an opportunity to redress the balance.

"Did you see her boobies?"

"Um . . . yes . . ."

"Good," snapped Night Rider. "Don't say anything now. Tonight, when everyone is together, you can describe the left boob. Got that?"

"Um . . . sir?"

"And tomorrow night, you can describe the right boob."

"Yes, sir!"

When not discussing women's anatomy at great length and their experiences with said anatomy in excruciating detail, Turtle began cultivating a patch of shrubbery the size of a dollar bill in the courtyard outside their living quarters. By giving it little drinks of water he transformed the fragment of dusty vegetation into an area of green measuring around two feet square. A sign beside it read: THE MAINE FOREST.

As autumn approached, the Mainers began to dream of days that began before dawn with a thermos of coffee drunk beside a trailhead or on the shoulder of a woodland road while the cold mist eddied around their ankles before spiraling skyward, and the rising sun lit the leaves still clinging to the tops of the trees. When the light reached the trees' trunks and the hunters' faces and the glowing orange of their hunting shirts, it was well and truly morning, and legal to begin stalking deer.

Iraq actually boasts a few species of deer—roe and fallow deer, not to mention oryx and some pretty gazelles—but none were seen at Abu Ghraib. Feral cats and feral dogs were perhaps the most visible mammalian wildlife at FOBAG, at least during the day. In theory these should have kept the rat population down, but their efforts (or perhaps their appetites) were self-evidently insufficient. There were a lot of rats.

When the bosses made it known that dead rats were the preferred variety at Abu Ghraib, the Mainers decided to translate a venerable Maine tradition and started a Big Buck Pool at the Mortar Café.

The carcasses of "harvested" rats would be hung on a pole in the courtyard as if prepared for gutting and cutting. Each was neatly labeled with the name of the hunter, the approximate weight and length of the rat, and the weapon with which the rat had been brought down.

For example:
SPC R. PARKER
BUCK [that is, male]
FOUR POUNDS, NINE AND A HALF INCHES
SIZE THIRTEEN MILITARY ISSUE BOOT

The guys at the motor pool adopted a feral kitten, which they named Hajji-Pussy, or HP for short.

Parker taught Lunch Lady how to play hackey-sack. They played for hours, toeing and heeling the little crocheted, rice-filled ball back and forth between them in the courtyard that served as the front porch and gathering place for First Platoon.

When they had first arrived at Abu Ghraib, that courtyard was a mess. It was littered with debris including a flattened soccer ball, bits of discarded clothing, plastic Iraqi prison-issue shoes, and a wealth of human bones. There were big bones, like fibulas and scapulae, and smaller ones, like phalanges and metatarsals poking intermittently out of the dirt. Some fragments of skull were still large enough to recognize. Most of the remaining skeletons likely had already been ground down, now indistinguishable from the omnipresent dust. Still, when the rains came, a faint smell of decaying flesh rose from the sticky mud, and Dizl insisted that the Lost Boys remove their boots when entering the living quarters.

"Just like the mudroom back home," he said, when they complained. "You're not tracking that stuff in here."

It was a strange and sorrowful thing to dwell amid these remnants of Saddam's victims. In the normal world, the compound would've been carefully excavated, the bones subjected to forensic examination and DNA analysis to determine both the truth of what had happened to their owners and to match them with grieving families. But Abu Ghraib was not and, realistically, never had been part of the normal world as the boys from Maine understood it. There was a gas chamber in their building and a room equipped with a permanently installed scaffold sized to accommodate two simultaneous hangings. Abu Ghraib was one big crime scene, one big mass grave.

Eventually, Dizl and the other soldiers began collecting the bones and setting them aside. In time, some of the bones in the growing collection seemed to match enough in size and general location to have come from a single person. Perhaps, once reassembled into a whole skeleton, this victim might be returned one day and answer the question, *Where has my loved one been all this time?* The Lost Boys called him "Frank" and kept him in a shoebox on the shelf.

At intervals, when someone discovered a new bone in the court-yard outside, Frank's box would be taken down and his bones laid out in their anatomical positions like a six-foot puzzle on the floor. Then, whoever would try and piece the fragments into gaps in the skeletal structure.

Such morbid games would come under scrutiny when the tenure of the 152nd coincided with a period in which the mental health of the troops at Abu Ghraib was being attended to with anxious assiduity, lest some overlooked mental illness provoke another efflorescence of misconduct and—not incidentally—scandal. Army psychologist Colonel Larry James had recently been dispatched to the prison to evaluate conditions and make recommendations to General Miller regarding both detainee mental health care and the maintenance of psychological well-being among the troops.

A swarm of shrinks, some from the Army, some from the Red Cross or other NGOs, but all with similar diagnostic and therapeutic ambitions, followed in the colonel's wake. One of these was a woman who, by appearance and in her heavily accented speech, strongly resembled Marlene Dietrich, at least to those soldiers old enough to know who Marlene Dietrich was.

Marlene, as she came to be known, took a dim view of some of the recreational opportunities created by the Mainers. She made it clear that the Big Buck Pool showed troubling evidence of a callous disregard for life. The fact that the rats were a risk to public health that had been specifically targeted for extermination, and if they weren't killing rats in Iraq, these soldiers would be killing deer in Maine, made no difference to the head shrinker.

She'd already expressed concerns about the mental stability of the Mainers to the command staff when, one rainy day, she happened by their hooch and discovered some of the Lost Boys hunkered down together on the floor with a shoebox full of bones opened beside them. They innocently explained to her that they were whiling away their off hours assembling Frank.

Apparently so appalled as to have lost the power of speech, Marlene stood mutely among the rows of muddy boots, her shoulder braced against the doorjamb as if she required its support to stay upright in the presence of such madness. She lit one cigarette from the butt of the last while watching Night Rider carefully arrange gray ribs on either side of a fragmentary sternum. "We're missing a clavicle," he announced.

"Is this a clavicle?"

"Dude, that's a coccyx . . ."

"You know, I think we've got an extra jawbone in here . . ."

From the doorway, Marlene rasped, in her thick, smoky, Teutonic voice, "This is not healthy." The boys looked up in surprise. "Truly," she lamented to the confused soldiers, "this is *not* healthy!"

It became a punch line in response to any number of "untoward" events. Perhaps a wrestling match went on for longer than observers felt was consistent with participants' claims of heterosexuality, or even upon receipt of news that a soldier's wife or girlfriend had cheated on him.

"Truly," they would shout with joyous condemnation, "this is *not* healthy!"

"FRAGO: DON'T USE THE BUG SPRAY." Command passed down word (rumor) from on high that the insect repellent the men of the 152nd relied on to keep at bay the litany of malaria-bearing mosquitoes, flies, and moths was toxic and they shouldn't use it.

Not only a nuisance themselves, the bugs attracted hordes of feathered and furred insectivores. Bats were one of the common insect hunters. A number of bat species native to the country, including free tails, mouse-tails, horseshoe bats, tomb bats, and pipistrelles flitted over Abu Ghraib's evening skies. No one thought to identify the species of bat that got stuck to Sugar's face, though.

The bat had flittered across the beam of a Humvee headlight and, disoriented, attempted to turn in the air. The onrush of the vehicle swept it into the cabin, where the poor bat found itself pinned against a strange, soft object that happened to be Sugar's face.

Sugar screamed and fell over backward, his hands clawing at his helmet. For a long, unpleasant moment, Dizl, who was in the truck, thought Sugar had been hit by sniper fire. That he had, instead, apparently been attacked by a rabid bat wasn't a whole lot better. Though the unfortunate bat was at least as eager to be rid of Sugar as Sugar was of it, the animal's head had gotten wedged under the front lip of Sugar's helmet, and all it could do was flap its wings helplessly at Sugar's cheeks and scrabble at his chin with its hind feet.

Later, Dizl would draw a cartoon for the 152nd's FOBAG news-letter, reinterpreting the ineffectual movements of the trapped bat as the manifestation of some strange interspecies amorous advance. Sugar was, after all, Dizl pointed out, probably pretty cute to a bat.

On being shown the cartoon, Sugar shook his head. "This is *not* healthy," he declared.

Allied soldiers weren't the only ones living in less than acceptable and mind-numbingly boring conditions. The quality of life for detainees at Abu Ghraib was pretty crummy too, especially at first. Some of them could alleviate the grinding boredom by making contraband, like the very useful hajji-hammer, or by making mushkallah (trouble) among themselves. They could beat someone up, always an attractive recreational option for some, although the Mainers were a whole lot more proactive about stopping fights than the previous guards had apparently been.

"I saw them fighting. I shot them. They ran like rabbits," Specialist Humpty said.

He was a man of few words, but an excellent marksman. The nonlethal rounds fired from Humpty's M16 would consistently sting exactly the right anatomical target—enough to distract, not enough to injure.

Presented with Humpty's *veni, vidi, vici* style of report writing, Beerboy tried tactfully to explain that his account of the incident wouldn't please the bosses.

Humpty gazed at his sergeant with his usual egg-like imperturbability. "That's what happened," he said at last.

"Well, I know, Humpty, but the bosses like to have just a bit more detail."

Then, wilting under the continued impassivity of Humpty's gaze, Beerboy dismissed him. With a sigh, he sat down and picked up his pen.

At 1640 hours on the northwest side of G-2, I observed Rachma 294055-A approaching Rachma 284492-D in an aggressive manner . . .

Occasionally, these fights became a team effort for guys like Lucifer and his compatriots. Riots occurred, though in general these were much more easily contained than they had been in the past. During one of these outbreaks of bad behavior, Lucifer got shot right between the eyes, though lucky for him the bullet was made of plastic.

With unusual docility, Lucifer approached Red, pointing to the black plastic tail fin that was sticking out of the bridge of his nose.

"God . . . OK. Hold still," Red said. He looked closely at Lucifer's nose, while Lucifer, crossed-eyed, tried to assess his situation. "No!" snapped Red, when Lucifer raised his hand to touch the thing. "Don't touch!" Red remembered hearing, somewhere, that the sinus cavity is separated from a person's brain only by a thin membrane. Clearly, this less-lethal round was stuck in Lucifer's sinuses, which had to mean that any untoward movement could be, well, lethal.

"We'll call the doctor," Red decided. He radioed to the Combat Support Hospital (CASH) and explained the situation to the lieutenant colonel/doctor who answered the call.

"Bring him down here," the doctor advised.

"Sir, I don't want to move him."

The doctor harrumphed. "All right. I'll come to you," he said.

For ten minutes or so, Red watched Lucifer anxiously. Lucifer didn't seem to be in too much pain. He was still on his feet, and showed no inclination to sit down, let alone pass out. The wound bled a little.

"It will be OK," said Red.

The doctor arrived, an IBA thrown on over his scrubs, and marched up to the detainee. "What've we got here?" He leaned in, adjusting his glasses for a closer look. "Huh," he grunted. Then he reached out and, with the air of a wine connoisseur pulling a cork, plucked the bullet from between Lucifer's eyes.

"You didn't want to maybe numb him up a little, first?" said Red, but the doctor was already marching back to the CASH.

"Put a Band-Aid over the hole," he advised over his shoulder. "Should be fine."

So Red put a Band-Aid on Lucifer's nose, applying antibiotic ointment first. He hovered around for a few days, calling Lucifer to the wire at intervals so he could check the man for signs of infection or brain damage, but Lucifer seemed to heal well. Soon, he was his nasty, vicious self again. What finally more or less cured Lucifer of his problematic and dangerous behavior was not being shot with rubber bullets, however unpleasant this near-lobotomy had been. Rather, it was the Red Cross–approved restraint chair the Mainers had built according to Maine State Prison specs. Two trips to the chair, combined with relentless professionalism and consistency, and Lucifer became voluntarily compliant.

Though, as Turtle observed, "he still hates out-of-staters."

Mostly the detainees structured their time around bathing their feet, hands, and faces before prayers, as well as the prayers themselves, offered in the direction of Mecca five times daily.

Snacks, too, were entertaining to acquire because it required some effort on the detainee's part (begging, swiping, bargaining) to convince guards to give in to their pleas.

Still, the basics of prayer, food, personal hygiene, and Count left hours in the day to fill, and some of the more ingenious detainees could've out-created MacGyver or Martha Stewart. Using only materials scavenged or stolen, they fashioned purses and shopping bags, weapons, and even a radio antenna made from a Styrofoam dinner plate, wires, and aluminum foil. One guy took his newly issued canary-yellow prison jumpsuit into his tent and came out wearing a three-piece suit that Turtle told him admiringly was "badass."

Sometimes, when a detainee left on the Happy Bus, they gave the homemade items as good-bye presents to the soldiers. Red received a box about the size of a Monopoly board that was exquisitely, intricately inlaid with minute bits of wood, glass, and pebbles that the detainee had collected from the debris of the prison and shaped laboriously using only handmade tools.

Another detainee smelted a nail in a campfire, shaped it, drilled it, and sharpened it until he had a needle that he used to embroider flowers, geometric designs, and sayings from the Koran into the plastic of empty MRE bags using colorful embroidery threads he'd carefully unraveled from scraps of cloth.

"Mister-mister! I have one spoon please? One spoon?" was a common request. In the hands of a skilled Iraqi crafter, an ordinary metal spoon could become a beautiful little belt buckle. Unfortunately, a spoon could also become a lethal weapon with little effort, so the guards were advised not to be generous with them.

Beerboy struck up a bit of a friendship with a dignified older detainee whose real name was Ali, though Beerboy called him Chief. This gentleman who, clad in a long gray shirt and red pants, somehow bore a strong resemblance to the thinner versions of Santa Claus, was an artist in real life. During one conversation through the wire, Chief asked Beerboy about the derivation of his nickname, and the sergeant explained that he and his father brewed beer in a small town in Maine.

"Ah! Beerboy!" said Chief. "So . . . I would like some, ah . . . colored pencils? I would make you a picture as a gift."

As he was scrounging up some colored pencils from the resident artist, Dizl, and cutting a piece of cardboard out of an MRE carton, Beerboy wondered whether he had talked too much. *Will Al-Qaeda in Iraq send hate mail to my family, or blow up the brewery?* he thought. *It's not as if it would be very hard to find, even with the minimal information I've given to this guy. Maine is small.*

He set aside distrust, however, and handed the cardboard and the pencils across the wire to Chief, who disappeared into his tent. After an hour or so, he came out, bearing his offering with shy pride. It was a drawing of a beer tankard sporting the classic cap of foam. The Arabic writing, Chief explained, said "Beerboy."

"Wow! Thanks!" said Beerboy, moved.

And then, because this was the way of things at Abu Ghraib, the sergeant brought the picture to another enclosure and confirmed the translation.

"What does this say?" he asked a random detainee.

"It says . . . ah . . . beer . . . boy?" the man replied, mystified.

"Good. *Shukran.* Thank you."

For a young man who hailed from a village in which many residents still don't lock their doors, distrust was an alien and uncomfortable experience. As it happened, al-Zarqawi never did turn up in his hometown, and Chief's gift adorns a wall in the brewery to this day.

For a time, detainee soccer was a distraction and was at least as tightly organized as the Maine coastal amateur's league in which Dizl played *hamy el hadef,* or goalkeeper. There were bitter contests for the championship, until the Americans discovered that the teams had been formed along sectarian lines (Shiites vs. Sunnis) and were mirroring the civil war that had begun beyond the walls and, sadly, had to put a stop to the games.

During the Great Sorting and subsequent relocation into Redemption, Shiites and Sunnis perforce had separate living quarters, though naturally it pained the idealists to do this. In the words of one famous American, "Can't we all just get along?" But the answer, at least in the short term, was no.

Though they shared an enthusiasm for soccer, if the descendants of Ali and the fans of the Caliphate were restricted to intramural play, the competition was less aggressive and injurious, and the post-game celebrations far less likely to end in fistfights and the subsequent discharge of nonlethal rounds from the towers.

THIRTEEN

GENERALS, COED SHOWERS, AND TAMPONS

"I didn't want to disappoint [Graner] just because then he'll leave me and I'll feel alone in this war zone."

—Interview with Lynndie England, BBC, aired August 13, 2009

A FEW OF the Mainers were in Tower G-7-1 one night, eating the most delicious ice cream from Belgium, of all places. The Iraqi night was calm; the men were happy and relaxed. It wouldn't last, however, and the peace was broken by the chattering thunder of a heavy machine gun squirting long streams of tracers at their tower.

The Bad Guys had snuck the gun up onto that ever-handy highway overpass. Tracer rounds that looked like flaming tennis balls snapped past the tower and the big bullets sounded like timbers snapping in half as they broke the sound barrier over Dizl's head.

But the Mainers kept eating the ice cream, hunkered down on the floor. The boot (new guy) was staring up at the tracers. His eyes were wide and his mouth wobbled around a scream. He wasn't eating his ice cream. So, giggling like school kids, Dizl, Parker, Red, and Turtle scarfed down his portion too as the strings of bullets snap, snap, snapped overhead.

They were National Guard troops stuck in a silly little wooden tower at Abu Ghraib, eating what they would afterward refer to as Belgian PTSD medicine. They were veterans. After what must have seemed like an indeterminably long time to the boot, Marines from K Company, recently assigned to protect the prison, lit the Bad Guys up, decimating their little group and making them pay for the indiscretion. The Mainers cheered and hugged and laughed.

They had all wet their pants, of course, but the new guy was the only one who was worried about it. He wasn't a veteran yet. He hadn't eaten his ice cream.

As the world foamed and raved over the photo scandal, General Miller arrived for another visit, if only so that news agencies could take pictures of the American brass marching muscularly around the prison with purposeful expressions. But the war was going badly all over the theater, not just at Abu Ghraib, and running detainee operations for a country that appeared to be in the middle of a meltdown couldn't have been easy for the general.

Damage control wasn't the only motivation for Miller's visits to FOBAG. In any event, on this particular occasion Sergeant Horton decided that the general and the press corps were marching through Ganci in such a way that the most disgusting and potentially lethal features of life there were bound to elude his notice.

"Goddamn it," Horton announced from his spot beside Dizl in the Hawk's Nest where they watched the general's progress through the prison. He got to his feet and headed for the stairs.

"What's up?" Dizl asked.

Horton paused and glared at Dizl from under his eyebrows. "The general is not going to see the shit."

"Huh?"

"General Miller needs to know about the shit. And you know what, Diz? Fifteen minutes from now, I'm going to be just like you."

"What are you talking about?"

"When I get back, I won't be an E-5 anymore, I'll be a forty-year-old E-1 private, just like you."

Dizl grinned. "Ah. Roger that," he said.

As Dizl watched, fascinated, from the Hawk's Nest, Horton proceeded to stalk the general as he and his entourage wended their way around Ganci. The wire fences formed a maze and Horton had a hard time figuring out not only where the general was, but what route he could take to be sure of intercepting him. Lacking radios, Dizl could offer no aerial guidance from his vantage point in the tower.

At last, by accident or providence, Horton found himself perhaps ten yards away from the general, separated from him only by the tall, chain-link fence topped with razor wire.

"General, sir," he called through the barrier. "Could I have a word with you, sir?"

General Miller turned. On the other side of a fence stood a barrel-chested, mostly eyebrows American sergeant. Behind the sergeant, and behind concertina wire, a large group of detainees gathered, perhaps anticipating a show.

"Sergeant?" the unsmiling general responded.

"Sir," barked Horton. "With all due respect, sir, the sanitary situation here is unacceptable. There is human waste everywhere. Look, sir," Horton said, turning over his boot for the general's inspection. "There is human excrement on the soles of our boots. The detainees are walking around in sewage. This is not acceptable, sir."

General Miller shot a sharp, sideways glance at a hovering subordinate.

"Thank you for bringing it to my attention, Sergeant."

"Sir!" said Horton. "Yes, sir."

As it turned out, Horton wasn't the only one who'd insisted on pointing out the discrepancies to the general. During Miller's meeting with the command staff, Huladog respectfully reminded the general of the standard operating procedure for detainees, or prisoners of war.

"Sir, I refer to the Five Ss," said Huladog, referring to field manual guidance of *search, segregate, silence, speed, safeguard.* "Given the frequency and intensity of enemy fire, it seems to me that we cannot claim to be providing for the proper *safeguarding* of these people."

This was not the first time Huladog had raised this point. Before the April attacks, the response was that the soldiers in FOBAG would just have to make use of what was available, but not to worry because, according to commanders, there were sufficient troops on the ground in the area to ensure the safety of all Abu Ghraib's inhabitants.

The second time he asked, they had already endured the April attacks, and the original answer was too obviously incorrect to deliver with a straight face. So this time, the general's staff told Huladog and the other officers about the plans already underway to transfer the whole detainee operation to the new Camp Bucca, already in place and being renovated and expanded.

This was probably not a lie, incidentally, though it was the most cheerful possible spin that Miller could put on the truth of the matter, which was that the accommodations under construction at Bucca would be sufficient to relieve some pressure at Abu Ghraib, but couldn't house the whole crowd. Perhaps, too, the general's staff was hoping that the more optimistic predictions about the Iraqi conflict coming from the office of the secretary of defense would prove based in fact rather than in politics, and Abu Ghraib would soon be unnecessary.

Still, in the meantime it was hard to deny the mortars or the shit on the soles of Horton's boots, and perhaps this is why Horton was not, as it turned out, demoted to E-1, although he was "counseled."

It all boiled down to poop. In 2004, one could divide the overall population of Abu Ghraib prison by the answers given to a single question: Where do you defecate?

According to a reliable informant, American civilian employees of the omnipresent Kellogg Brown & Root had genuine, porcelain flushing toilets in their trailers while soldiers and detainees did their business in porta-potties.

These needed to be pumped out at regular intervals if they were to remain "fresh," or at least to prevent them from actually overflowing. So periodically a flock of little tanker trucks would arrive at Abu Ghraib, pump out the porta-potties, and take the contents away to be disgorged into what one can only hope was an environmentally sound lagoon in the southeast corner of the prison grounds.

The soldiers on duty in the Ganci towers could see, and sometimes smell, the lagoon seething and bubbling beneath the desert sun. As the moisture evaporated, the pond, dubbed Shit Lake, developed what Dizl and the Lost Boys referred to as a *puddin' skin* thick enough for the smaller feral dogs to skitter across its undulating surface.

"Does anyone check the shit trucks?" Dizl asked one day, as he and Turtle sat sweating in the tower.

"Check the shit trucks? What for?" asked Turtle. He was peeling the wrapper from a package of peanut butter crackers. He offered one to Dizl.

"Insurgents. Bombs. They come through the gate empty, and no one looks inside." Dizl chewed.

"Who's going to want to check? Have you ever smelled one of those things?"

"There is a rule when working in a prison. If you can see it, those hundreds of other sets of eyeballs have already seen it and they have a plan. Your job is to disrupt their plan."

"You think the insurgents have a plan for the shit trucks?"

"I'm saying that if you were an insurgent, you could hide a bunch of guys with guns in one of those tanks. Once through the gate, you would all bail out and start blasting. Like the Trojan Horse."

"I would be so nauseated from being in the tank I wouldn't be able to do anything but puke," Turtle pointed out. "Wanna Twix?" he added.

Dizl took the Twix and conceded, "Still, someone ought to check the trucks."

Nearly all the guys had chronically bleeding rectums, probably due to the cumulative effect of the chow, the germs, and the strenuous desire to have one's business done as swiftly as possible before a mortar landed on them and an army chaplain would have to inform their mother or wife that their loved one died on an overflowing plastic toilet.

Baby wipes, sent from home, helped a little. However, several Americans learned the hard way to check if their wipes were for human use and not disinfectant; an application of bleach or cleaning products hardly soothes a burning anus. On the other hand, a wipe enhanced with aloe vera could be downright luxurious.

One of the perks of riding a convoy to Baghdad was the opportunity to use a toilet that wasn't subject to mortars or rocket fire.

"Hey, Diz," Parker asked one day. "Where were you yesterday?"

"Went to Baghdad, to Brigade HQ."

"How was it?"

"There was a real toilet," Dizl replied dreamily.

In the courtyard outside the Mortar Café, the soldiers could wash their uniforms in a set of automatic washers that strongly resembled the toy appliances sold to children. Imagine the laundry equivalent of an Easy Bake Oven, with a similarly toy-like capacity and power, as if whoever manufactured the things was afraid the soldiers might hurt themselves with a real laundry machine, or even a bucket-and-mangle.

Then there was the matter of where one bathed. There was a shower trailer, the kind you see at construction sites. It had five shower stalls and sinks for hand washing and tooth brushing, but the one at FOBAG had many large holes in it. While this was a problem for privacy, it also made it a little too obvious that the shower trailer was as armored as an empty beer can. It is difficult to enjoy the experience of showering, naked, in a fiberglass shower stall when a bullet or a mortar might come punching through the wall.

Seeking some protection from the snipers and exploding shells, the Mainers tended to prefer the hard shower located down in an old torture chamber plumbed with makeshift, but effective, piping. The water came out of pipes above stalls demarked by cheap plastic shower curtains. Given the least encouragement, these would wrap themselves around the shower in a clammy and surely germ-laden embrace.

There were no drains either. The wastewater simply flowed across the floor and out into the corridor, where it disappeared into a crack in the concrete so deep that Dizl was sure it dribbled all the way down to hell. The hard shower was fetid and spooky, but at least there was concrete between a naked self and the mortars. This was a psychological asset more than anything; plenty of concrete walls and roofs at FOBAG had impromptu windows and skylights punched in them.

The shower was coed, which hadn't bothered the men and women stationed at FOBAG. It was like camp or the coed facilities college students have in their dorms. It was not especially uncomfortable.

Then the smart people from Big Army got involved. They didn't want to risk having anything at FOBAG that could have any potential of turning into a problem resembling sexual harassment. The photos of naked detainees simulating blowjobs still sat in the front of every commander's mind.

So the FRAGO came down: "NO MORE COED SHOWER-ING! And while we're on the subject: NO URINATING IN THE SHOWER!"

"God! I can't believe this!" Humpty groaned, upon reading the "DON'T PISS IN THE SHOWER" sign, as if yet another basic human right had been snatched away from him.

"Remember the three-hour rule," Dizl said helpfully. "Maybe it'll change back."

The powers at "Shadow Main," the headquarters of Abu Ghraib, actually wanted the hard shower closed down and disassembled. Huladog responded with the requisite "roger that" and proceeded to dutifully ignore the order.

Instead, he worked out a male/female shower schedule to accommodate the needs of the few women dwelling nearby, and convinced the KBR water deliveryman that, despite loud brass sounds to the contrary, it was still OK to refill the tank.

"If you get caught doing it, I'll take the blame," he said reassuringly. As the ubiquitous refrain had it, "What can they do to me? Send me to Abu Ghraib?"

Home may be where your heart is, Dizl mused, *but FOBAG is where our hearts, brains, guts, spines, and balls are. The priority is keeping them all connected to each other.*

Dizl didn't think "balls and ovaries." Of the 124 members of the 152nd FAB, none were female. A field artillery battalion is considered a front-line combat unit and therefore not open to female soldiers under the ban against women serving on the "front line."

On the other hand, MP units do include women, and the units from Ohio, Pennsylvania, and Puerto Rico deployed with the 152nd at Abu Ghraib had a few female soldiers in their complement.

This presented some predictable issues. When some female MPs took to sunbathing on the roof of the Mortar Café, for example, the chopper traffic over the building became so thick that the women were asked to desist, for reasons of safety. Though, as a grateful Dizl pointed out, the hovering helicopters tended to suppress enemy fire, no small benefit for all concerned.

A diminutive, redheaded Pennsylvanian added a welcome touch of feminine energy to FOBAG life when she befriended a number of the Mainers. Dizl and Red nicknamed her Shirley because she resembled the perky character on the TV sitcom *Laverne and Shirley*.

Shirley was energetic, kind, and funny as hell. She taught a detainee nicknamed Jackie Chan to do the chicken dance, and she was a favorite with the juveniles. Though she would bristle when described this way, the Mainers thought Shirley was adorable.

She lived in a prison cell at FOBAG. She liked the relative security of bars on the doors and concrete walls all around her to keep out most of the mortars.

She had a total of three roommates at Abu Ghraib. Of these, two became pregnant and were sent home. The first one was pregnant before she left the United States; the other became pregnant while at Abu Ghraib.

"People are still people no matter where they go," Shirley said to Dizl.

Despite the standing "no sex in a combat zone" order, the staff at the clinic found that, to their surprise, the courtesy jar of condoms needed to be refilled far more often than the courtesy jar of candy. However, with birth control usually being one of the many details often overlooked in moments of passion and pregnancy being a ticket out of a deployment, it meant soldiers were "still people," and mistakes happened.

The only shortcoming to Shirley's quarters was that the cell wasn't in the basement; what makes a dungeon makes a sanctuary. Well, that and the lack of anything resembling indoor plumbing. However tedious it was to up-armor for yet another schlep to the porta-potty, peeing in a bottle wasn't an option for Shirley.

A plastic box the size of a phone booth heats up to sauna temperatures under the savage Middle Eastern sun. The smell is downright offensive even in the best of times. When there was a siege on and the KBR pumper trucks stopped coming, the toilets smelled like the end of the world.

To make female hygiene and bathroom practices even more complicated, the whiteboard outside the command post offered daily warnings about burning personal correspondence and anything else that might compromise the already fragile operational security at FOBAG, which included used tampons. This naturally made a woman wonder: what use might al-Sarawak make of the knowledge that the female soldiers at Abu Ghraib were on the rag?

When one was crouching in the porta-potty, nose instinctively burrowing behind the ineffectual mask of one's IBA collar, head whirling from the combined effects of heat and a refusal to inhale, the safe, secure disposal of a pearlized plastic tampon applicator seemed borderline impossible. Years later, Shirley could still be awestruck by the unassuming feature of American life that is the toilet. The gleaming porcelain surfaces and elegant, sculptural lines, the satisfying waterfall sound it makes while rinsing everything away, were no longer basic necessities but luxuries.

Adorable and generous, Shirley's mother sent a care package once a week filled with treats and personal hygiene items, enough so that Shirley was a frequent contributor to the "Take It If You Need It" shelf in the supply room.

Shirley, to the chagrin of male and female politicians, was one of thousands of women serving in Iraq in 2004. In fact, the Center for Military Readiness, a nonprofit educational organization that openly opposes allowing homosexuals to serve in the military, also aims to limit the number and career choices for women in the military.

There are members of the armed forces who continue to argue against women in combat roles, claiming they aren't mentally and physically strong enough. Some organizations believe that women are more prone to erratic or violent manners when under the stress of surviving a "man's world."

"There is no excuse for what happened at Abu Ghraib," declared Elaine Donnelly, the founder of the Center for Military Readiness. "I am disturbed by the role that a few female soldiers played in it. It seems that a gradual but sweeping degradation in civilized values is happening before our eyes. No surprise to me, since we are forcing women to compete in the ultimate male world, the world of war, which is anything but civilized," suggesting that the presence of women at the prison was a contributing factor to, and maybe even the cause of, the abuse on Tier 1-A.

Women serve as soldiers and Marines in harm's way. This can be accepted cognitively and yet still shock the heart when, for example, a feminine name jumps out from the list of the year's dead. The ban on women engaging directly in front-line combat missions has been rendered moot by the predominance of insurgent and terrorism-based warfare in our time. According to the Department of Defense, as of 2014, 958 female service members have been wounded and 152 have died while serving in Iraq and Afghanistan.

What Donnelly laments, the degradation of civilized values that comes from the equal participation of women in traditionally masculine spheres, attempts to exclude women from responsibility for evil using nineteenth-century misogynistic cultural rules. This is not uncommon.

When one mentions the surprising number of women who took starring roles in the Abu Ghraib scandal, female friends sometimes grow defensive.

"Well, but these were women who were trying to get by in a male environment," they explain. "They were trying to fit in, they had to prove themselves, show they were just as tough as the boys. They couldn't rock the boat!"

However, putting the responsibility of the abuses by the "fragile female soldier in a man's army" on their male compatriots detracts from the participation of women like Shirley in the project of Redemption, which was not a matter of genes and hormones but rather of a determined, daily decision on the part of an individual, male or female. Their goal was to show their enemies—unarmed in cages—compassion.

It is Lynndie England's leash that lets us know who Shirley is. Shirley is the one who had the strength to actually bear the burden of moral responsibility, of strength and compassion even in the face of evil.

FOURTEEN

GROUNDHOG'S DAY

"On Monday, about 400 prisoners were set free—more than half of a planned two-day total of 640 releases, military officials said. . . . [M]any of the detainees said Abu Ghraib was not the same prison it was when reports of abuse by US guards surfaced more than a month ago.

'The Army is good now,' said Satr Sim Mohammad, 23."

—"For Freed Iraqis, Mixed Emotions; Many Leaving Abu Ghraib Cite Improvements Since Scandal," *Washington Post*, June 15, 2004

TWO ROCKETS LANDED on the roof above Red's room and exploded.

He had been sleeping on his back, hands resting on his chest, thumbs locked, which was always how he slept.

"You look like you're ready for the coffin," Sugar remarked once, to which Red simply answered, "Well, I might as well be."

The first explosion woke him, and when he turned his head instinctively away from the loudest noise and opened his eyes, there was an orange glob of molten metal—part of the housing from the rocket—stuck to the wall next to his head. He could feel the heat on his nose.

He leapt up and had time to strap himself into his body armor and snatch his rifle off the hooks on the wall before the second rocket exploded and blew him out of his door and onto the floor of the hallway.

The hall was filled with smoke. Red could feel the effort his brain was making as it sent forth messages, telling the heart to keep beating, imploring the legs to get moving, but the legs were ignoring these. Or maybe they, like Red himself, couldn't hear anything.

A familiar face materialized out of the smoke. It was his friend, the diminutive Marine who went by the nickname of Gunsmoke.

Gunsmoke's mouth was opening and closing with some violence. *What's he doing?* Red wondered.

Shouting, of course.

Red shook his head and pointed to his ears.

Gunsmoke tore open Red's vest, reached inside it, and ran his hands over Red's stomach and around his back. *What the hell?* Gunsmoke withdrew his hands and checked them for blood. He refastened the body armor, looked up, caught Red's eye, and gave him an exaggerated thumbs-up.

Ah. No holes in me. That's good.

Gunsmoke's mouth was moving again, "We've got to get out of here."

Red shook his head and pointed to his legs, *They don't work.*

Gunsmoke frowned. *That's bad.* Then he shrugged, grabbed hold of the strap on the back of Red's ballistic vest, and dragged the big man briskly down the hallway to safety.

The concussive force of the explosions had bruised the inside of Red's spinal column, producing an injury that is a variation on a traumatic brain injury. As it turned out, once the initial swelling went down, the brain's messages could get through, and sensation returned to Red's legs. To this day, they still have shaky, painful moments.

Once Gunsmoke had seen Red safely into Chiclets's hands, he dashed back into the still-smoking LSA and retrieved Red's family photos from where they were still pinned on the splintered walls of his room.

"The shrapnel chewed 'em up a little," he said apologetically when he handed them to Red. "But you can still see their faces."

It was just another day at the 'Ghraib.

Skeletor stopped by Tower 2 in Ganci 4 one day to have a chat with Major Payne who, when not standing guard duty, filled the important role of FOBAG barber. From the tower, Skeletor saw a group of detainees behaving strangely. One man began beating the bottom of an upside down trashcan with a stick while the detainees around him began to chant and dance.

"Staff Sergeant," Skeletor said into his Motorola. "The guys in 4 are doing some weird sort of tribal thing here."

"Check?"

"They're drumming and dancing around."

"I'll come over and take a look," said the staff sergeant.

"Roger that."

"Do you think it could be the signal for a riot?" asked Payne nervously.

"That stick is large enough to use as a weapon," Skeletor replied thoughtfully.

Below them they saw Tex, now recovered from being rocked by the mortar attack, arrive at the wire and beckon to Firos, the translator, and to Abu Hussein. The compound chief approached the wire smiling.

"No mushkallah," Hussein said reassuringly.

Firos explained, "It is a religious celebration, Captain Tex."

"What are you using for a drumstick?"

Abu Hussein called the drummer over to the wire. The drummer held his drumstick aloft for inspection and Tex saw it was the bottom section of a crutch.

Tex laughed. "Does this mean some poor guy is doing without his crutch?"

Hussein pointed to one of the tents. "It's OK," he said. "No mushkallah."

"All right, then," Tex said. "Party on."

He went up the stairs to the tower, where he and Skeletor and Payne watched the drumming and dancing. At length, the drumming paused and Hussein said something to the others. They turned to the tower and waved their thanks at Tex.

Tex waved back.

Flushed with exertion and the joy of their celebration, the detainees gathered around the base of the tower and shouted "Tex!"

Tex threw up his arms.

"*Tex! Tex! Tex!*" the detainees chanted. Tex threw up his arms again, and they all cheered and laughed. It turned into an impromptu celebration of its own, the staff sergeant throwing up his arms, the detainees chanting, everyone laughing, the drummer pounding out a syncopated accompaniment. For all of these men, living amid the mortars and concertina behind the walls of Abu Ghraib, it was a much-needed moment of sheer, silly joy.

Rioting was a real threat, and while the excitement of the celebration didn't escalate beyond a fun party, ideology, pent-up frustration, or sheer boredom could erupt in violence that was often directed at other prisoners. In August, two prisoners were shot dead during a riot in the worst episode of internal violence in months. Five prisoners had already been attacked and injured. Something had to be done to quell the brawl before they could be rescued from the compound, so the soldiers at first tried to control the crowd with variations on the saying, "drop the fucking rocks," then with less-lethal rounds (rubber bullets). At last, a soldier from Pennsylvania opened up with his shotgun.

Yogi arrived just after the gun went off, in time to oversee a doomed effort to resuscitate the two detainees who'd sustained mortal wounds from the lethal shotgun blasts. Yogi would be haunted by the episode. He felt responsible ("Well, we are responsible for these people, aren't we?" he pointed out to Dizl) for not managing to arrive at the scene in time to somehow make it turn out in some other, better way. This burden was made heavier by Yogi's belief that the wrong guys had been shot. "These were the guys who were usually trying to help us out," he pointed out. "They weren't the instigators."

"I don't think the Pennsylvania guy knew them," Dizl said.

Yogi shook his head. "I should've gotten there sooner," he said.

There was an older teenager, perhaps seventeen, who Red nicknamed Shriek. A skinny kid with an electrified frizz of wild hair, in an American school system he would undoubtedly have been classified as ADHD and appropriately medicated. As it was, he had spent a few months as the leader of an insurgent mortar team and he had killed many people—though the number was almost certainly exaggerated—which he clearly thought entitled him to the fearful respect of the other kids in his compound.

As his leadership tended to consist of tormenting some kids and winding the rest up for misbehavior, Shriek was a bit of a problem. And if all that wasn't bad enough, when mortars were falling, he had the irritating habit of postponing his retreat into the safety of the new bomb shelters until one of the soldiers had threatened him. At that point, he would move indolently toward the shelter where the other kids were already huddled, offering his all-purpose English-language commentary on his world.

"Mortars are good!"

Red was very tired of the hyperactivity, the bullying, and the ostentatious slow walk to the bomb shelter.

So the day came when—*Krumpboom!*—a mortar fell, and then another, and Shriek smiled at Red and said, "Mortars are good." He was just turning to begin his slow, contemptuous shuffle to the bunker when Red flung the gate wide.

"Get over here, kid," he said, clutching Shriek by his shirt. Red pulled him out of the compound and marched him briskly into the alley between the compounds. *Krump!* Another mortar fell, this one a little closer. In the middle of the flat, dirt alley stood the steel cage used as an isolation cell for Level Five detainees who just weren't getting with the program.

"What do you want me to tell your mother, kid?" Red asked Shriek as they approached the cage. "I mean, when she comes to Abu Ghraib to pick up your body: What do you want me to say to her?"

He unlocked and opened the door to the isolation cell with one hand, keeping hold of Shriek with the other. *Krump!* Another mortar. It was definitely closer. He pushed Shriek into the cage.

"Huh? What shall I tell her?"

Red stepped into the cage after Shriek, slammed the door shut, locked it, and threw the keys out through the wire. "You want me to tell her that mortars are good?"

Krump! Krump! Shriek was down on the ground now, curled into a ball, yelling. *Krump!* Red was on the ground too, curled up next to Shriek so his body might shield his, but he was still yelling in the kid's ear: "Mortars are good? Is that what you want me to say?"

Krump . . . Krump . . . the mortar attack went on for twenty minutes, perhaps half an hour. It seemed longer. When it was over, Red picked Shriek up and set him on his feet.

"Listen, kid," he said seriously. "In a couple of weeks, you're going to be eighteen, and that means you won't be the big kid in the little kids' compound, you'll be the little man in the men's compound. You have to decide how you're going to handle yourself, and I'll tell you right now, if you keep acting the way you do, you aren't going to do very well."

"OK," said Shriek weakly.

"No more 'mortars are good,' OK?"

"OK."

And Shriek was a pretty well-behaved boy after that. It wasn't too long, anyway, before it was decided that Shriek could be discharged, presumably into the bosom of his family. When he was boarding the Happy Bus, he handed Red a present. It was a long strip of fabric.

"From the tent," Shriek said, and grinned. As he and Red both knew, this material was contraband in itself, as the guards took a dim view of prisoners who damaged prison property. On this strip of fabric, Shriek had carefully written, in passable calligraphy, his name in Arabic and English.

"Ali Abu Neda," Red read aloud.

"Yes," said Ali. "That is so you don't forget me."

In June, two simple words saved lives: "kill" and "them."

The ROEs still in place did not permit the soldiers or Marines on the ground to make independent decisions about what did and did not constitute a threat. Something that didn't look right—the guy skull-fucking you with his binoculars from the overpass, for example—had to be phoned in to "Shadow Main" and approval obtained before countermeasures could be taken.

One evening, two vans approached the main gate to the prison. The Marine at the gate called the command post inside, and Lunch Lady picked up the phone.

"Sir, two vehicles are approaching at a high rate of speed."

"Kill them," said Lunch Lady, and the Marine opened fire.

The vehicles, loaded with explosives, detonated, killing one Marine, but the blast occurred far enough away that the gates were not breached, as was the intention.

It happened that Horton was outside the wall that evening, and when he heard the explosion, he also ignored the ROE, which would have required him to fall back inside the prison. Instead, he charged into the fray and fought beside the Marines, earning himself another "adverse counseling" session with superiors outside his unit and the enthusiastic gratitude of the Marines themselves.

Military leaders later decided Abu Musab al-Zarqawi, the swaggering, self-appointed, "pathologically brutal" representative of Al-Qaeda in Iraq, instigated the attack.

He'd named himself after a youth spent in the Jordanian city of Zarqa, but his friends called him al-Ghraib, "the strange one." Al-Zarqawi was responsible for the bombing of the UN headquarters in Baghdad that killed twenty-two people and led to the withdrawal of the United Nations from Iraq. He deployed suicide bombers for another massacre of pilgrims in Najaf and Karbala in December of '04, and had made the provocation of sectarian violence a personal project. As if all this weren't enough, in the vicinity of FOBAG, al-Zarqawi was the head of the head-choppers, personally decapitating at least a half dozen people for the benefit of web-surfers worldwide.

The local garbage pickers—line workers in the ubiquitous third-world recycling program—found and sold paperwork to al-Zarqawi that bore the names of officers, or envelopes with names and return addresses still legibly inscribed.

So the Secret Squirrels would pass along reliable HUMINT that al-Zarqawi had put a price on the head of this or that officer at FOBAG, and there were wives and husbands back home in Pennsylvania and Puerto Rico who received hate mail from al-Zarqawi's operatives. "*We know where your husband is,*" the letters would say. "*We know where you are.*"

Then there was the memorable moment when one of the most docile, compliant detainees of Ganci 4 was headed for home and planted his flip-flop–shod foot onto the step of the Happy Bus, turned to Turtle, smiled, and said, "I hear Maine is very nice this time of year. I shall go visit your family."

This was the source of Beerboy's fretfulness about Chief. Even if he eventually decided to trust that Chief was OK, this offered no reason to abandon a more generalized paranoia. Huladog reminded his Mainers, again and again, to destroy their paperwork. Horton shredded his and then burned it for good measure while thinking of his wife and daughters on the other side of the world, whom he loved with a passion that his time at Abu Ghraib had only purified and made plainer.

One day, a few of the Lost Boys were "tasked" with taking a small convoy of trucks to BIAP. This wasn't an unusual occurrence. There were many reasons for Abu Ghraib personnel to travel beyond the relative safety of the prison walls. A detainee scheduled to make his case at the Iraqi provisional court in the Green Zone; a soldier whose injury or illness was more than even Chiclets's skills could manage, or whose mental health issues might benefit from an hour of talk therapy (albeit bracketed with couple of hours of extremely stressful travel); someone heading off for home leave from BIAP, or someone who needed to be picked up and returned to FOBAG; escorts for valuable men or matériel—all such expeditions required a minimum of three up-armored Humvees to counter the risks posed by IEDs and ambushes.

For some, shepherding a convoy was a welcome opportunity to get out from behind the walls of FOBAG and take a gander at the towns, people, and farmlands surrounding the prison.

Though very little of Iraq's land is viable for agriculture, what exists is concentrated in the area around Baghdad, with water from the legendary Tigris creating a zone of vegetation that gives the scenery a Floridian look. Irrigation canals meander past fields and plantations of date palms, and the Tigris flows green when seen from the seat of a passing vehicle but is revealed as an astonishing, tropical turquoise when viewed from a helicopter.

Fields of barley and wheat glow golden in the sun, and farms boast rows of lush plants laden with tomatoes, cucumbers, and chickpeas. Children would appear along the roads, having learned to expect a shower of candy from American Humvees. When the natural cosmetics company Tom's of Maine sent over a case of toothbrushes, Dizl took to tossing these to the kids, who to his amusement generally reacted with the comical disgust of young American trick-or-treaters offered apples instead of candy corn on Halloween.

The excursions to Baghdad would've been idyllic, in fact, if it weren't for the roadside bombs, the heavy objects and explosives dropped from the overpasses, the snipers and rock-throwers, and the gigantic craters and bullet pockmarks that scarred the buildings and palaces of Baghdad.

On one memorable occasion, Dizl was driving a truck that chose a bad moment to shed its serpentine belt. Immobilized for what was probably five minutes but felt more like so many hours, Dizl and Beerboy waited for the rest of the convoy to turn itself around and return to the rescue while, all around them, Iraqi MMAs (males of military age) responded to this targeting opportunity by making ominous cell-phone calls.

Travel was dangerous. This was the reality that brought Huladog to the staging area to see the convoys off, and again to welcome them home, all smiles, while his eyes moved from face to face, assuring himself that all his guys were back, and whole.

By this point in their deployment, the Lost Boys knew the route and the routine. They drove in a manner that would give any Maine State Trooper an aneurysm. The key to avoid getting hit was high speed, weaving back and forth over the median and into oncoming traffic to avoid possible VBIEDs, and veering violently when any object larger than a cigarette packet was spotted beside the road.

Dizl made sure that Lenny the Lobster accompanied him and the other soldiers on their convoys. The plastic lobster would sit on the dashboard next to a can of Moxie soda to help remind the soldiers of the 152nd of their home.

Before setting off on one particular convoy, they received intel that would make them even more jumpy and leery of civilian vehicles. Insurgents had begun driving high-performance sedans packed with explosives into the middle of military convoys before detonating. Before setting out, Dizl made sure to remind his guys of the rules of convoys that were much like the rules of the middle-school lunch line: *No cutting.*

A substantial concrete barrier, with one Humvee-sized opening left to accommodate traffic, defended the main route to BIAP. Iraqi civilians used this opening as well, and soldiers were sometimes posted at it, making the opening an occasional impromptu checkpoint. The Mainers' Humvee, number two in a line of three, darted off the main drag and made the left-hand turn through the barrier without slowing down. It was your basic up-armored lefty at thirty miles an hour through a twelve-foot gap in reinforced concrete.

As the lead Humvee cleared the opening, a white van with a group of Iraqi men inside attempted to make a thirty-mile-per-hour right-hand turn and cut in line between the lead vehicle and the Mainer's gun truck.

"Hey! *No cutting,*" Dizl heard himself shouting as the adrenaline spiked his heart rate and tunneled his vision.

Lunch Lady, at the wheel and already flinching in expectation of an explosion, accelerated. As the driver, Lunch Lady's vehicle would serve as his weapon, and his goal was to smash the van and its occupants into the concrete barrier. Meanwhile the gunner, Roy-Roy-the-Naked-Boy, swung the Humvee's roof-mounted machine gun around to bear on the white van.

"*Ramming!*" shouted Dizl.

"*I'm gonna shoot!*" shouted Roy-Roy.

"*Oh, fuck,*" someone yelled.

Just as Roy, Dizl, and Lunch Lady were about to unleash hell on the white van, Dizl noticed something was off about what they were all sure was a VBIED about to send them home early.

"Wait!"

As it turned out, the men in the white van were not terrorists. They were just a group of national-civilian workers who had made a gross error in line etiquette. Luckily for them and everyone involved, the van's driver slammed on the brakes. As the Humvee hurtled past, the soldiers caught a glimpse of the occupants, displaying the appropriate bug-eyed, wide-mouthed screaming and hand-flailing body language of people about to be crushed and machine-gunned to death by those crazy Americans from Abu Ghraib.

Dizl turned in the passenger seat to check Lunch Lady's well-being and saw the same bug-eyes and the open mouth. He probably looked that way, too.

Meanwhile, Roy-Roy-the-Naked-Boy was jabbering in adrenaline-infused war lingo from the gun turret. "*Yeah,*" he yelled. "*Take that, motherfucker. Did you see that, Lieutenant? Hey, Lieutenant, did you see that? Whooo-whee! Git some!*"

They dropped off their passenger at BIAP, stopped by Brigade HQ to take care of some small errands, and then made a drama-free run back to Abu Ghraib. Huladog was there at the gate to meet them, counting their heads with the subtlest movement of his calm brown eyes.

Protocol was to fuel up vehicles before returning them to the motor pool, so Dizl drove their Humvee around to the fuel point. The KBR civilian contractors—the ones Roy-Roy, wide-eyed, had once described as "men from places with monkeys" (an accidental bit of racism, perhaps, as the contractors were from "exotic" places like Africa)—came out of the shade to work the gas pump.

The wall that rose behind the fuel tanks stood perhaps twelve feet high. It was made of the usual grayish-brown reinforced concrete, and on the other side of its illusory protection lay the living quarters for the Lost Boys.

His heart rate still slightly elevated, his perceptions sharpened by the neurochemistry of near-tragedy, Dizl saw a cat. Stretched out on the wall, perhaps to dry in preparation for tanning, was the freshly rugged-out pelt of a large, orange cat.

Dizl's first thought was: *Garfield!*

And then came realization: "Holy shit!" he said out loud. "They ate it." *The KBR guys ate the cat!*

After that day, Hajji-Pussy wore a little kitty-collar that, in indelible Sharpie, someone wrote "Pet of the 152nd FA. Please don't eat."

FIFTEEN

SMOKES AND SANDBAGS

"[Sergeant Hazen] said the daily life inside the prison is eerily similar to what's happening outside the walls. . . . It's a constant game of cat and mouse, just like the constant killings, kidnappings, and bombings bouncing between Mosul, Fallujah, and Baghdad."

—"We're At Abu Ghraib To Make Things Better,"
Camden (Maine) *Herald*, September 28, 2004

AFTER ONE PARTICULARLY close call with an exploding rocket or mortar ("I could never tell the difference," he said) Dizl found himself lost in a childhood memory. He stood on Main Street in Thomaston, Maine, eating an orange-pineapple ice-cream cone. He wasn't called Dizl then, but Kelly. He was in the fifth grade, a blond boy who had to punch a kid to prove that Kelly could be a boy's name, too. With him at the ice-cream stand was a little girl named Wendy. Their desks had been side by side in third grade at the St. George School, where Dizl had been happy. But Dizl's mother had fallen in love with an ex-convict who married her, and they moved to California. During two terrible years on the West Coast, Dizl and Wendy had written back and forth to one another, and by the time

Dizl and his mother finally escaped from the ex-con and returned to Maine, he was ten years old.

"I love you," he said to Wendy, after he finished his ice cream. He meant it.

Decades later, while he was in Iraq, Dizl received a care package from Wendy. It contained the book *Life of Pi*, and Dizl read it again and again, as if it were the Bible, because it was good and because it had come from her.

The original plan was that they were all supposed to go home in November, but—FRAGO—the 152nd got "extended" for three months.

In Washington, DC, there were public-affairs specialists whose assigned task was to scour the Internet for any news report that contained the words "Abu Ghraib" in any of its various spellings. Thus, though he didn't know it, Beerboy's superiors had been apprised, from Washington, of the remarks he had made to his hometown newspaper back in Maine before he was even back in Iraq from R&R.

Huladog heard about it first. Adjectives like "unhelpful" were used, and nouns like "counseling" as well. Beerboy was not, in fact, disciplined, and he owes it to the intervention of his first sergeant.

In particular the higher-ups were displeased with Beerboy's assessment that the United States was "in the wrong country, fighting against the wrong people."

"I'm proud of what I'm doing, but I hope this is all worth it, men and women giving their lives for the cause," the story quoted Beerboy as saying. "I stand behind what I'm doing, but I don't want to be a statistic and I don't want to be a flag on the lawn in Rockport."

"That wasn't helpful," said the captain.

"The sergeant is a citizen-soldier, sir," Huladog pointed out, placing a deliberate emphasis on the word "citizen." "As such, he retains the right to express his opinion when he is on his own time and in his own home."

The captain said unhappily, "The people at Victory and in DC are concerned that our men do not understand the gravity of the situation."

"Given that we are faced inside the walls and outside by Islamic extremists who want to kill us, sir, I believe my men fully understand the gravity of the situation. They do not require perspective management from Washington."

Huladog was tempted to add, but didn't, that Beerboy did not need advice from a lot of anxious armchair warriors who didn't have to begin the day wondering if they'd be KIA by suppertime just because they took too long to have a bowel movement.

Who would have imagined that a piece in a newspaper only a few hundred people are ever going to read, in a state most Americans think is part of Canada, could inspire so much interest from these guys? Huladog asked himself, amazed.

A photograph accompanied the newspaper article. It was a shot of the mailbox that stands on its post outside Beerboy's family home. In the picture, the mailbox is patriotically decorated, the cheerful scarlet-and-white stripes of the American flag glowing against a backdrop of cerulean sky and lush, vivid green grass and trees.

"I hadn't realized how much I missed color," Beerboy admitted.

"I'm not who I was," Dizl declared to Turtle one day. They were wriggling into their body armor with reflexive eagerness, having been startled from sleep by an explosion.

As if this were the only conversation to be expected at such a moment, Turtle replied, "I know. I'm not who I was, either."

For one thing, muscle memory allowed each man to finish strapping on body armor, check the firing mechanisms of their rifles, and begin evaluating his environment for tactical defensive and offensive possibilities before the comparatively sluggish processes of his conscious awareness had even registered a threat.

While useful for survival, the changes in the human brain brought on by prolonged exposure to a hazardous environment carve grooves so deep in one's mental pathways that the brain only knows how to function in a war zone. Our bodies do not lightly or easily discard lessons illustrated and emphasized by danger.

After the first mass casualty attack in April, Dizl became downright obsessive about the number and arrangement of sandbags in the Hawk's Nest. He would pen his paeans to a sack of sand, its simplicity, its earthy good looks, the way it crunches slightly as it supports a resting elbow or a braced foot, and, above all, its yielding, all-forgiving nature. It just lies there, absorbing rain, absorbing shrapnel, and absorbing at least some of the concussive force that would otherwise snap a man's aorta or batter his brain. You can keep your drones, your nukes, your satellites: Here is a device with so many military applications that the only limiting factor is a lack of human imagination or perhaps an insufficient will to survive.

When Parker, book in hand, arrived one morning to find that the side walls of the little "room" at the top of the tower had been raised by a foot or so of sandbags, he gave Dizl a resentful look.

"I know," said Dizl.

Parker said it anyway. "If the walls are higher than my head, I can't watch the hajjis over the top of my book. I'll have to stand up, like you."

It was true. Dizl spent a lot of his time in the Hawk's Nest standing, pacing, pondering the tactical possibilities of what he saw laid out before him in Ganci. He had left gaps to serve as rifle ports in the sandbag walls, but these were neither large or numerous enough to allow Parker to use them for ordinary surveillance purposes.

"You can rearrange the bags on your watch," Dizl conceded. "You can take 'em down altogether if you're so inclined, but when I come on watch at 1200, I want these walls to look exactly like this; the same number of bags in the same places. You got that?"

"Roger that, Private Major," sighed Parker.

As it happened, it was these carefully arranged sandbags that saved Dizl's life on April 20.

As the rainy autumn approached and the 152nd moved operations over to the new site at Redemption, Huladog pointed out that while twenty inches of dry sand will stop a 120mm round, you need twice as much wet sand to get the same effect. Dizl gazed at his first sergeant, his face puckered.

"Roger that," he said, and went out to find more sandbags.

Filling sandbags is a task requiring little in the way of skill or even strength, so it was one of the employment opportunities frequently offered to detainees. Americans often offered payment in the form of cigarettes, with a premium placed on American Marlboros, though a larger quantity of Iraqi "Miamis" could be grudgingly accepted instead. In fact, Beerboy discovered that in the micro economy of Abu Ghraib, a single Marlboro menthol was worth a whole pack of Miamis.

Cigarettes, incidentally, were the usual motivator bored detainees would offer Thumby as an incentive when they wished for him to create some entertainment, say by flinging himself headlong into a large coil of razor wire.

Once, when Thumby was preparing to perform just such a stunt, Dizl arrived and threatened, very credibly, to shoot Thumby rather than put everyone through a lot of gory nonsense. The rounds in his shotgun weren't lead, but rather the small, less-lethal plastic rounds. These seldom caused real injury, but could usually generate a sufficient sting to discourage further mischief. The sound made by the racking of any round, lethal or otherwise, into the chamber of a shotgun tends to focus even a madman's attention.

"Come on, Sesma," said Dizl, holding out his hand. "Come away from the wire. I'll get you some cigarettes tomorrow."

"Marlboros, not Miamis," said Thumby, and Dizl shook his head and said fine.

Sesma was Thumby's real name, the name Dizl had asked for one day.

"I am Thumby," said Thumby.

"No. That is not your name. What is the name your mother gave you?" Dizl insisted, and Thumby got a faraway look in his eye and in a small, almost-sane voice, responded, "Sesma."

While cigarettes may have been parceled out with what the detainees considered excessive frugality, there was no scarcity of the basic raw material for making sandbags. And, once the long-overdue portable bomb shelters had been placed in the enclosures, detainees got downright enthusiastic about reinforcing these with stacks and stacks of sacks of sand.

As long as the sandbags they filled were destined for their own use, there was no problem with having the detainees while away the hours of incarceration performing this task themselves. However, the rules of war forbid an occupying power from setting prisoners to work in ways that benefit the occupiers, so they couldn't make sandbags for the Americans.

The Americans had another pool of labor they could potentially tap for sandbag manufacture. Among the varied sorts of people collected together at Abu Ghraib was a group of about twenty Somali men. The typical appearance of Somalis is tall and thin, and thus they were known as *Skinnies*. They dwelled in their own enclosure and, though their living quarters lay behind wire fences, the Skinnies were not technically considered detainees. They were non-Iraqi nationals who had had the misfortune of being in Iraq as guest workers when the occupation began. They stayed behind fences because, for some reason, no one made plans to send them back to Somalia.

So they remained, snoozing in the shade of their tents and playing cards, and once they had filled enough sandbags to satisfy their own safety needs, they showed no inclination to fill any more, at least not gratis.

Perhaps, the command staff suggested, the Somalis could be hired to fill sandbags? They proposed the idea to the Somali leaders.

"How much?"

A negotiation followed. Eventually the Skinnies and the Americans made a deal that included a sum of cigarettes, candy, and other desirable commodities, and the Somalis arrived in the courtyard of the Mortar Café to begin work.

A few days went by, and the piles of sandbags grew. The vulnerable window openings of the Mortar Café began to seem at least a little less like open invitations to mortar rounds.

Then word came down from above that the Skinnies' sandbagging operation must cease and desist.

"Really? Why?"

"It looks bad."

"What looks bad?"

"We're Americans. We've got history on this."

"You mean like from Mogadishu? Black Hawk Down?"

"No, dummy. I mean slavery."

"We're paying them!"

"I know that. You know that. But from the outside, it looks like a bunch of whites lying around while the blacks do the work."

"But sir, they don't have to work . . . they're getting paid to work . . ."

"I'm just saying. It looks bad."

What if a reporter took a photograph and put it on the Internet?

They solved the problem by making sure that whenever the Somalis were filling sandbags, one of the Americans (it had to be a white American—a black American wouldn't do at all) sat there and filled sandbags too.

SIXTEEN

KAMAL

"I couldn't help but say to [Mr. Gorbachev], just think how easy his task and mine might be in these meetings that we held if suddenly there was a threat to this world from another planet. [We'd] find out once and for all that we really are all human beings here on this earth together."

—President Ronald Reagan, 1985

WHEN DIZL WAS, perhaps, five or six years old, he came across an article in an old, yellowed *National Geographic* about the cave paintings at Lascaux. He was unable to read yet, which probably intensified the visual dimension of the experience of looking at an image in ancient charcoal of human figures jabbing spears into a creature that looked like a big, hairy rhinoceros.

In that instant, as he sat there on his Gram's couch, the entire drama flashed before his mind's eye in full Technicolor, DreamWorks style; it was both the moment when the power of visual art declared itself to him, and the first time he experienced the squirt of adrenaline and the slowing of time . . . *one thousand one . . . one thousand two . . .*

that he would later encounter in battle, all because of a picture of a picture.

As he got to know the detainees better, Yogi, like Dizl, wondered if some of what he had done—the scorched helmet act, for instance—might have contributed to the problem rather than to the solution.

It's a trickier question than it sounds. On the one hand, there were certainly people arriving at Abu Ghraib who really couldn't understand any incentive to restrain aggression other than a show of superior force by an absolute, implacable, and even slightly insane authority figure. This was what they knew, the form in which power had always been wielded in their world.

Someone accustomed to being yelled at, beaten, threatened with death or with the slaughter of his family, and who has, in his turn, threatened and done all of the above to others will not be able to engage in a reasoned conversation about shared values and common understandings. Civil dialogue is a learned skill, and the Detainee Inprocessing area at Abu Ghraib prison, circa 2004, was not an optimal learning environment.

If, instead, the incoming detainees were given a six-foot-three, two-hundred-forty-pound American with crazy blue eyes and a flaming helmet, the ordinary ones might be traumatized, but the scary head-choppers might just be intimidated enough not to get themselves or anyone else killed that day.

But then there was Kamal.

Kamal was fifty-four years old, a round-faced, mustached man. He stood just over five feet tall, and on a good day might have weighed about a buck and a half. When the detainees had their showers, they were given razors and some simply shaved off clean, but Kamal always took care to trim his mustache carefully, as if to keep himself who he was.

Kamal arrived at Ganci on the day of the Flaming Helmet, together with a group of a hundred or so other men, the result of a sweep conducted after allied troops found insurgent weapons in their village.

Because Kamal was seen as a leader in his community, the Americans presumed that he must have known of the cache and thus, silently at least, supported the insurgents.

This Kamal would deny in his conversations with Yogi, and Yogi was inclined to believe him. If the insurgents deigned to inform Kamal of their presence in the village, Yogi figured, such communication would certainly take the form of a threat: *We are here. There is nothing you can do about it. Give us a hard time and we will kill you and your family.* Thousands of civilians who'd been kidnapped, tortured, bombed, shot, and beheaded lent mute endorsement to such claims.

Unlike Ganci, Camp Redemption, Kamal's home for the foreseeable future, was deliberately and carefully organized. The layout of the new enclosures recognized and emphasized the distinctions that could be made between the dangerous detainees and those simply in the wrong place at the wrong time.

Redemption had five basic levels of detention. Detainees who were dangerous, violent, and inclined to fight guards or murder fellow prisoners found themselves sequestered at Level Five. The lowest risk folks lived at Level One.

Upon arrival, everyone, with some exceptions, was placed in Level Three for thirty days. During those thirty days, guards would monitor the detainees for risk factors and behavior. Depending on results, they'd send new arrivals up to Level Four or down to Level Two.

All personal possessions were taken away from the detainees when they got to Abu Ghraib, leaving them with a jumpsuit, a bedroll, and a pillow. When a detainee was moved to Level Two, some of those possessions would be returned, and he might have limited visits from family members. If his behavior allowed him to qualify for Level One, he would have more of his own stuff back, and more visits, maybe his infant daughter handed over the wire to be dandled and shown off to the others, maybe a moment's embrace. Eventually, if he was cleared for discharge, he would be taken to a small tent camp set up on the former site of Ganci to be "out-processed" and sent home on the blue-and-white Nissan diesel Happy Bus. Together with the other men caught up in the sweep, Kamal had had his possessions taken away, including his own clothes. He had been given a canary-yellow jumpsuit to wear, and had the rules and systems of Redemption explained to him by the large American with the smoking helmet and the ice-blue eyes.

He would see the man with the ice-blue eyes often and have ample opportunity to observe him, to watch his interactions with the other Americans and with the detainees. One day, perhaps two or three weeks after Kamal arrived, he approached Yogi and introduced himself, in English.

Kamal regarded the Mainer for a moment before he calmly announced, "You do not want to kill me. I know this about you."

"Well," said Yogi, an honest man, "I would if I had to."

"Yes, but you do not want to," said Kamal.

"No, I don't," Yogi admitted, and Kamal nodded.

They would go on to have wide-ranging conversations over many months, talking through the wire about families and children. The familial conversation was limited to Kamal's family, not Yogi's. It was considered seriously unwise to give any personal information to any detainee, however kindly. They talked about what they might have been doing if the war hadn't happened, what they might like to do when it ended. Even this first encounter would, in retrospect, be viewed through a lens adjusted by the beginnings of their mutual regard. Kamal was more than a foot shorter than Yogi, but Yogi would always remember seeing eye-to-eye with him. In fact, if anything, Kamal was taller. In the Mainer's memory this Iraqi stood out from the other men as Mount Katahdin stands out above the low hills that surround it.

Kamal projected the gentle energy of a man who is entirely at peace with himself, and is disposed therefore to regard anyone he encounters with a kind of friendly interest. He had an openness to engagement that was rare among those who have been arrested and imprisoned.

When Kamal was placed in Level Two and able to receive family visits, Yogi would see his wife arriving punctually every week to visit him. They'd learned, though, in "cultural sensitivity training" that it would not have been appropriate to greet her. Between visits, Kamal sent letters home to her, which Red occasionally dropped into the command post mail bin to be read and evaluated by the Secret Squirrels before joining Iraq's burgeoning postal system.

How is it, Yogi wondered, *that this man doesn't loathe me? We have made life so hard for him and for his family.*

He saw Kamal's wife making her way down the alley toward the cages, her burka flapping gently around her invisible ankles. He watched his friend's face until Kamal's radiant smile told him that Kamal had spotted her too.

However, no matter how much Quantock and his men had improved it, Abu Ghraib remained an unpleasant and dangerous place. There were legitimately threatening people, criminals, and insurgents held there. Including, in fact, some of the same people who had cached weapons in Kamal's village and threatened his family. Kamal was afraid of such men and, knowing this, Yogi went out of his way to keep a vigilant eye out for mushkallah that might come near him.

So Yogi was very, very happy when the word came that Kamal had been cleared to go home. He brought the news himself.

"Ah," said Kamal.

"It's great, isn't it?" said Yogi enthusiastically. "You'll get to see your wife, your family, your kids, and your friends."

Kamal didn't seem excited. His face was grave. "What about you, my friend? I will not see you?" he asked.

"No," Yogi said. "No, you won't see me. You will go home to your wife, and soon I hope that I will go home to my wife. And I will be glad to know that you are home and well."

"I, too, will be glad when you are home," Kamal said sadly.

Kamal boarded the Happy Bus. Some of the newly released Iraqis hung out of the windows, laughing and joking as they waved good-bye, but Kamal remained quiet. The Happy Bus, fully loaded, lumbered off with a rumbling entourage of Humvees and armored trucks. Yogi waved until it turned the corner, and smiled because the whole idea of homecoming sounded so sweet.

A few days later Yogi was supervising the arrival of visitors and spotted the familiar figure of Kamal's wife approaching Redemption.

Oh no! Did we put Kamal on the wrong bus? Maybe she was away from home and doesn't realize he isn't here?

Kamal's wife was scanning the faces of the soldiers around her, clearly looking for someone. When she spotted Yogi, she immediately approached.

"I am Kamal's wife," she said, surprising him. For some reason, it hadn't occurred to Yogi that she, too, could speak English.

"Yes, I know," said Yogi. "Listen, you do know that Kamal has been sent home, don't you? He left three days ago."

"He came home," she said. "And the very night that he arrived, the insurgents came and shot him in the head."

Yogi, stunned, stared at her. He must have eventually said something, though he would never afterward remember what. Perhaps he said, "Oh no!" or "Are you sure?"

"Yes," she said. "They told us he had collaborated with the Americans in this place. They shot him in front of all of us. In front of his family."

Speechless with grief and horror, Yogi looked at her, then down at his boots, then at her again. She looked back, her brown eyes meeting and searching his blue ones.

"I have something for you," she continued quietly. She reached into the folds of her burka and pulled out a small, silver-colored chain necklace. From it dangled a thin, metal charm in the shape of the country of Iraq. "I want to give this to you. I would like for you to take it home to your wife."

"Ma'am, you don't have to . . ."

"This was given to me by Kamal when he was courting me. He wrote me letters from this place, and he told me about you, that you were a kind man and his friend."

"Ma'am, I don't know . . ."

"So I would like for you to bring this home to your wife. I want your wife to know that there are people here, in Iraq, who loved her husband."

Some European house sparrows that lived in the brickwork of their LSA befriended Dizl. Dizl was a bird-watcher, so they provided a comforting diversion. When he observed the birds, he thought of his grandmother and also of James Bond.

Not the spy, that is, but a well-known ornithologist who, believe it or not, had served as the namesake for the hero of Ian Fleming's *Casino Royale*. Besides having been a fan of Bond's bird books, Fleming apparently thought his was a superbly ordinary name for an extraordinary British spy.

Dizl had met Bond at the Gasparilla Inn on Boca Grande Island off the western coast of Florida, where Dizl drove a laundry truck for a time. He often thought of him and the interesting conversations they might have had if the aged ornithologist mimicked the spy and turned up at Abu Ghraib.

Abu Ghraib's sparrows liked to perch on a wire near a building that housed one of Saddam Hussein's torture cells. This room, with its tiled walls and floor, had no plumbing but boasted a big brass drain in the floor. There were two iron hooks in the ceiling, where Baathist dungeon masters would hang two friends or relatives from opposing hooks for torture. When it rained, a horrible smell would crawl up the brass drain.

This room became Dizl's art studio for a brief time. He made many drawings of the sparrows. "When you are trapped by duty or situation, in a hellish place," he explained to Red, "the notion of having wings can consume you."

One day, Sergeant Major Vacho showed Dizl a military challenge coin.

For those unfamiliar with this part of military culture, a challenge coin is a medallion about the size of a silver dollar that you carry in your pocket, which usually depicts the unit's name, logo, and some motivational drawing of war or the various scary animals that serve as symbols and nicknames. The idea used to be that if you are sitting in a bar and another veteran "challenges" you, you can show him or her your coin, and he or she has to buy you a beer. If you forgot the coin in your other pants, then you've got to buy them the beer.

While few contemporary service members have even been "challenged," or attempted a "challenge," the coin itself has become something of a collector's item. Marines, for instance, will show off coins passed to them by the commandant or sergeant major of the Marine Corps on tidy desk display racks.

"Do you think you could design one of these for Abu Ghraib?" the sergeant major asked Dizl.

"We don't have any art stuff, Sergeant Major," Dizl pointed out.

"Sketch something up, and we'll see what happens."

"Adapt and overcome" applies everywhere.

So Dizl went to talk to Jiffy-Lube at the motor pool. After considering the issues for a few minutes, Jiffy-Lube rooted around and found a piece of transparent Plexiglas about the size of an old record album cover.

This Dizl made into a light table by laying the Plexiglas across his knees and bracing his army-issue flashlight between his feet so the beam shone upward. It worked surprisingly well, at least during hours of darkness, and the drawings Dizl made on the computer paper Huladog supplied were the beginning of what he designated the Abu Ghraib Combat Art Initiative.

The design of the coin took Dizl a few days of deliberate thought, even as he sat sweating out his watch in the Hawk's Nest. The iconography wasn't the hard part: Shemis, the sun god and source of overwhelming heat (yes, yes, it's a dry heat) obviously should be featured, along with the omnipresent towers of FOBAG.

As he thought about the project, another image kept surfacing, submerging, and resurfacing in Dizl's mind: the image of a female soldier giving a happy thumbs-up next to a dead detainee in a body bag. The world had seen the photo, the Mainers of the 152nd had seen the photo, and they bore the weight of knowing what the world now thought about them and their service. *This is what we are up against at Abu Ghraib. Those photos, and what they represent.*

Restoring America's honor was the mission of the 152nd, and so *Restoring America's Honor* would be the *E Pluribus Unum* for the challenge coin. Long before Rumsfeld, or the Tea Party, laid claim to the phrase, it presented itself to Dizl as he sat amid the sandbags in Tower 7-1 through the long, hot, slumberous hours of the noon to midnight watch.

After completing the midnight ritual of trading places with young Parker, Dizl walked slowly back to his LSA. He was eager to get to his combat light table and start working on the lettering for that hook, Restoring America's Honor.

Pausing by the fuel point, he became aware that dark human figures were scuttling and hustling among the buildings, motivated by mortars to move quick and stay low. A helicopter full of Marines clattered overhead. It was a QRF (quick reaction force) battering its way through the sky, off to chase the Bad Guys and forestall explosions.

The rhino knocked the shit out of us and everything else, Dizl mused. *Finally, someone had the bright idea to sharpen the sticks.*

He experienced a sudden, strong desire to meet the family of the real Ganci, the fire chief who died on 9/11. He wanted to show them the coin he would design, show them his drawings, tell them about Redemption. He wanted them to know, wanted *everyone* to know, that there was honor and great love associated with their name.

At Abu Ghraib, the Great Sorting steadily reduced the numbers of detainees, releasing the innocent or apparently innocent, sometimes a hundred or more at a time. More and more, those that remained would be indisputably insurgents, foreign fighters, and dangerous persons, and thus could be expected to excite less sympathy among the Americans holding them.

Shirley could generally be found supervising the checkpoint at the entrance to the Hard Site. "High value" detainees were neither confined nor interviewed by Americans at the Hard Site by this time, and the portion of the building still under US control provided a safe, secure living space for the few remaining female prisoners. Shirley's supervisor was an E-6 so unfairly handsome that the Lost Boys had nicknamed him Sam Spade, Male Model, though for short they called him Spade.

Shirley was a friendly person, and she had grown up with brothers and been in the military long enough not to be flustered by the presence of even so impressive a specimen as Spade.

They got to know each other well, in the way that people do who spend twelve or fourteen hours a day together, sometimes for weeks at a time. It took Shirley a while to notice that Spade was supervising her AO with what struck disinterested observers (Dizl, for example, and Yogi) as excessive diligence. In the end, Spade's persistence paid off and Shirley eventually began to take him seriously. It helped that he was kind and capable, and also that he smelled good.

It's hard to imagine wooing in the context of Abu Ghraib, what with the sand, the spiders, the sweaty uniforms, and the frequent bouts of a dysentery-like condition that the Lost Boys referred to as JMA, an in-group acronym standing for "Juicy Man-Ass."

Still, one day Sam Spade kissed Shirley, and that was that. They fell in love.

"We will just tell people we met in prison," Sam Spade told her, laughing.

There was something comforting in the thought of two good people finding one another and so, in some sense, finding *home* in a bad place. If they were lucky and stubborn, Spade and Shirley would be able, always, to share not only the bond of committed spouses but also the bond of comrades who have shared the shattering experience of war. All in all, Dizl thought, Spade and Shirley were to be envied.

That some men and women (or men and men or women and women) had extramarital affairs with one another while at FOBAG should not surprise anyone with the slightest acquaintance or sympathy with human nature.

By the same token, no one should be astonished to hear that some soldiers at Abu Ghraib received the unwelcome news that their stateside spouses, bored by sacrifice and exhausted by solitude, were exploring other relationship options.

However, anyone with the energy to gin up moral indignation about the adultery, fornication, and other "self-soothing methods" that doubtless blotted the records of many American soldiers at Abu Ghraib has no possible way of understanding that, to those on the ground, these indiscretions were simply dwarfed by the huge and consequential moral questions that cried forth from that place and time, and echo still.

SEVENTEEN

R&R

"What a cruel thing is war: to separate and destroy families and friends, and mar the purest joys and happiness God has granted us in this world; to fill our hearts with hatred instead of love for our neighbors, and to devastate the fair face of this beautiful world."

—Robert E. Lee, letter to his wife, 1864

FIRST SERGEANT NOTES
For 13 September 2004

PLACE IN BURN BOX WHEN DONE REMEMBER!
Weather: Today 100 down to 70. Winds at 5–15 knots. Next two days 102 to 70 and 102 to 70.

Sun up 0645, down 1912. Moon up 0517, down 1853.

MSRs—Closed till tomorrow. Still some guys running around with car bombs.

CONVOY LESSONS LEARNED—As you all may know, SGM Butler's convoy was hit with an IED. His vehicle rolled three times. Your Platoon Sergeant has his AAR. Read and heed.

UNIFORM CHANGES—OK, here we go again. Your Platoon Sergeant has this list. See him for more details. No Arabic writing anywhere.

KBR—Lost three more workers yesterday executed and kidnapped. You may see a degradation of services around here similar to that which we experienced in April. Conserve drinking water. We may have to include spraying down the porta-potties and cleaning the other shower area in our daily cleanup.

WHEN ATTACKED—You defend from where ever you are at. If you are at the DFAC, you defend from the DFAC. Do not run back to the LSA or the compounds. If you're at the compounds, keep the detainees in. If you're at the LSA, stay in the building and follow the directions of whoever is in charge there. Don't go on the roof or start shooting outside the LSA from the inside. Get with your Platoon Sergeant for more detailed information.

ROE—Colonel Thomas has said that if you observe a bad guy violating the ROE (like a local in the back of a pickup with a machine gun mounted on the back) you can shoot. You don't have to wait for permission from Shadow Main. Follow the theater ROE for outside the compound when outside the compound, and the levels of force for inside the compound.

2D PLT AREA—When they leave, that area is to stay vacant. Do not move into any of those rooms.

EXTRA STUFF—All the extra items and stuff you may have acquired while here will not all fit in the conex boxes we will have to go home. If you want to start mailing some stuff home, I would start to consider that now. Expect to be leaving or selling the furniture and large items you have here if you can't mail them home. Also, expect there not to be many "someones" to sell them to, if we're here to the end.

The Iraqis were now managing the Hard Site where ordinary prisoners spent their days. The Hard Site had its own, exterior tower, manned by Iraqis who, from this vantage point, had a splendid view of everything that went on in the prison. They had clear lines of sight and fire on the helo pad, the DFAC, the front gate, the fuel point, the convoy staging area, everything.

Al-Zarqawi would boast, before his death, of having had spies well placed at Abu Ghraib. Dizl, for one, doesn't doubt that one or more of the Iraqi guards might have been among these.

Given the manifold and uncertain threats facing coalition forces throughout Iraq and around Abu Ghraib especially, it might have been wiser to delay handing over the Hard Site to the Iraqis. Certainly, as it turned out, the prisoners themselves would come to prefer the custody of Americans, who were, though this would not be advertised on Al Jazeera, considerably more restrained than their poorly paid and ambiguously motivated Iraqi counterparts.

In any organization, the decisions made by managers are often inexplicable to those on the line. Indeed, orders from above frequently strike subordinates as plain stupid even when the results aren't potentially lethal. Sometimes those decisions *are* stupid, based on misguided theories without sufficient appreciation of the facts on the ground. Sometimes the orders given by a superior officer are based on orders given to him by his own superiors, and so on up the line like a game of telephone with sometimes deadly consequences.

When the generals told the 152nd that Iraqis were taking over the Hard Site, Dizl and the others heard, "You will let the Iraqi Police put potential spies on the outer perimeter of the Hard Site where they will be able to view our entire operation from a commanding, elevated position, and yes, they will be allowed to keep their cell phones."

No matter how they interpreted them, the command staff on the ground at Abu Ghraib could not disobey such orders, nor even publicly question the wisdom of those who gave them. For Dizl, Huladog, Tex, Beerboy, and the others, *improvise, adapt, and overcome* was combined with *do not make us look bad.* Meanwhile, they had their own priorities, like making sure everyone marooned at Abu Ghraib, good guys and bad, made it home in one piece.

Home—Maine, that is—the people, the landscape, the normal sights and smells of it, the feel of your child's hair beneath your tousling hand became memories so exquisite that a man would instinctively place them in some locked mental cupboard, lest the longing they provoked in him become too excruciating to bear. The reality of Abu Ghraib was what was most important. It demanded complete attention. What remained on the other side of the looking glass would have to wait and fade into relative obscurity.

Sent home for a week or ten days of leave, a soldier wouldn't have nearly enough time for his mind and heart, attuned to the urgencies of war, to adjust to the peaceful priorities his family and friends would so eagerly press upon him. He wouldn't have time to disconnect from Abu Ghraib, and the fact that he would soon be returning made him disinclined to try. Comfort means complacency, and complacency kills.

Perhaps it isn't quite so odd, then, that nearly every soldier sent home on leave during his time at Abu Ghraib would, upon his return, respond to the question "How was it?" with "It was awful. I wish I hadn't gone."

When Dizl's grandmother died, though, he needed to go home for the funeral. Gram had been the constant of his childhood, the love of his earliest life.

Huladog pulled some strings and made a space appear on a C-130 flying out of BIAP. A number of soldiers then risked their necks driving Dizl down the runway so he could catch his plane; they were brothers, willing to face death so their comrade could make it home and say good-bye to a loving family member.

The C-130 lifted off and flew the way they do: straight up, cork-screwing into the sky, just like in a war movie. Wayne Newton and Kenny Chesney were on the plane too, for some reason. When they landed safely in Kuwait, Dizl told Wayne Newton that his Gram had been a fan.

The closer that he got to home, the more distant he felt from it.

Dizl's wife and young son met him at the snowy Bangor International Airport, a place that seemed library-quiet after the din of Iraq. *I am a ghost,* he thought, as he greeted them. He submitted to their kisses, but could not feel their presence. It was like being trapped in a glass room, separated from the family he had missed so much by this foggy, glass-like numbness.

During the week he was in Maine, he went hunting. He sat in the woods, listening to the familiar but unfamiliar birdsongs, inhaling the familiar but unfamiliar scents of pine and crushed fern. He saw a deer. It was within range, standing still, looking at him with its soft eyes, its big ears pricked and alert, but he didn't pull the trigger.

He chose not to shoot because he could, knowing that there might be a time he wouldn't be able to choose *not* to shoot a detainee when he returned. It'd already happened when Dizl had had to take a shot at a detainee to save the life of another. Three pissed-off prisoners were beating on a fourth with large metal tent poles. Dizl lined up the front post of his shotgun at the space in the fray where his first target's head kept popping up. He aimed just below the chin. Even with a nonlethal round, a shot to that tender spot would certainly kill the man.

The shot went high, though; instead of killing the attacker, it hit him on the top of the head and scalped him. Dizl shot the other two in quick succession. By the time he got to the last attacker, he and three other MPs had all lined up their shots, and the rubber buckshot from multiple guns all hit the man at the same time. It looked to Dizl as if the troublesome detainee had been swatted to the ground by a powerful fist.

He didn't *have* to shoot the deer. Dizl wanted to keep the choice to commit violence his during a time when he often did not. He had no reason to shoot the deer other than for sport and he knew he'd soon be returning to a place where he might be required to take a life in the line of duty. Nothing required him to shoot the deer, so he didn't. He was hunting, home safe in Maine, and, perhaps, wanted to avoid violence just as long as he could.

Later, he went to his little boy's soccer game in the town of Hope. As he stood on the strange grass in the strange, cold air, a former neighbor approached.

"Well, Kelly Thorndike!" she exclaimed. "Where have you been hiding yourself? I haven't seen you in ages!"

"I'm serving in Iraq, ma'am," Dizl replied.

With surprising speed, the woman's demeanor changed from sociable, playful interest to chilly disapproval.

"I'm a pacifist," she snapped. "I believe we should love our enemies."

Dizl watched his little boy's hands move in the air, his little boy's feet running across that strange, cold grass.

"Last week I bathed and fed an al-Qaeda terrorist," he said.

They had his Gram's service. He and his wife took their son to the beach, where the little boy threw rocks into the salty water with a mittened hand. The half-frozen sand squeaked beneath their boots. *Pretend the snow underfoot is sand,* the instructors at Fort Dix had said a lifetime ago.

In the nearby woods were little dens packed with nestled chipmunks, and larger dens where the local coyotes hunkered down, sharing the thick, gray-gold comfort of their fur. Even *thamnophis*, the garter snake, would be gathered with its fellows in communal nests called *hibernacula* where they pass the Maine winter, sheltering in the twisty embrace of other snakes.

When the time was up, Dizl's wife and son took him back to the quiet little airport in Bangor.

TSA agents flagged Dizl as he went through airport security. His dog tags, fastened to the laces of his combat boots, set off the metal-detector. They asked him to remove the boots for inspection; this was around the time that the shoe-bomber had struck, and the Department of Homeland Security was just beginning to get obsessive about footwear. So Dizl sat down on the floor to take the boots off. The line of people behind him halted to wait.

As he sat on the airport floor, his back to the glass partition between the security area and the waiting area, his little boy saw him, approached, and pressed his face against the glass and tried to kiss him. His mother, Dizl's wife, knelt beside the boy. She was crying.

Dizl couldn't hear them, though he knew they were saying something. He reached out his hand to touch his son's face, but of course he couldn't because the glass was in the way, a physical manifestation of the distance about to be between them again.

Meanwhile, one of the passengers in the line that had formed, waiting for this soldier to take his boot off, turned to the woman behind him.

"Do you know why they keep their dog tags on their boots that way?"

"I don't. Why?"

"It's in case they get killed and can't be identified by their faces."

Then everyone in the Bangor Airport security screening line began to cry.

For his last flight, Dizl took the quick hop in a C-130 from Kuwait to Baghdad. It was a short ride, perhaps twenty minutes. There were a few new guys on the plane, and Dizl couldn't help but notice, with some ambivalence, that they were all decked out with new state-of-the-art body armor, nice helmets, add-ons that protected the neck, the eyes, the balls. Dizl didn't have any of this. He had his desert camouflage uniform (DCU) and planned to pick up his old stuff at BIAP.

No new stuff for me, he thought, but then at least it appeared that the higher-ups were starting to get the messages about what soldiers in Iraq really required. As the plane began its approach and descent, one of the crew came back to inform the passengers that flights in and out of BIAP had been getting shot at all day. "So if you've got stuff, put it on," he said.

The kid in front of Dizl began buttoning up, doing up the Velcro, getting his gear on straight and snug.

Won't do you any good, Dizl thought. Then he was saying it out loud. "That won't do you any good, kid. The bullets they're shooting at us are going to be big as cucumbers and if one comes even near you it'll take big chunks off of you, and the plane will crash in a fiery ball, so adapt and overcome, kid."

So saying, Dizl took a pen and wrote his blood type on his arm. "B-POS."

It wasn't the first time he'd done this, though at FOBAG, he generally wrote it on his stomach.

The plane lurched and veered. "The way the pilot is flying, they probably are shooting at us," Dizl said. He handed the pen to the soldier. "Welcome to Iraq."

The kid began to pray.

The numbness and detachment clung to Dizl, only lifting as he got closer and closer to the 'Ghraib. Driving down the highway from

BIAP, he even felt a surge of well-being at the sight of a familiar green highway sign. The bottom of it had been cracked off in some volatile exchange, but it was still legible. In Arabic and English it said ABU GHRAIB, and an arrow pointed helpfully toward the off-ramp. When he came through the gates, there was Huladog, a permanent and comforting fixture for returning soldiers. The Marine was smiling with his mouth while his dark eyes checked Dizl over, checked him in: *Good. You made it.*

At the Mortar Café, Willard hugged him. "Glad to have you back, Dizl."

Dizl felt OK then.

One of Dizl's hardest memories from his year in Iraq isn't even from Iraq. It's the memory of being at the Bangor airport, untying his boots, his wife's weeping leaving him unmoved. It's the memory of putting out his hand to touch his son's face, and feeling only glass, and the fact that, even now, he still feels as if he loves everyone this way, with a barrier in between, and he fears he always will. It is one of the many prices he paid to survive.

Back at FOBAG, Dizl heard about Kamal, that the friendly man had been sent home on the Happy Bus only to be murdered in front of his family. Dizl regarded Yogi's loss and experience with unease.

In most prison entry-level classes, candidates are instructed about the importance of being fair and impartial. It's hard to do, but it is what can make the difference between imprisonment and correction. A personal relationship between jailer and jailed can produce any number of results, few of them good. This is true in Dizl's experience as a prison guard in Maine. He found it doubly true at Abu Ghraib.

Dizl didn't see Kamal the way Yogi did. For one thing, Dizl spent more time physically removed from the prisoners, so he was able to maintain more emotional distance. Cynically, he wondered whether Kamal was, in fact, a Bad Guy, one who had played Yogi (who, despite his fearsome mien, was a tenderhearted man), manipulated him to get what he wanted—protection, visits, information in, and information out.

Or maybe Kamal was just as he appeared to Yogi, a genuine, good human being who had been sustained in prison by his love of his wife and his friendship with an American with whom Kamal had a genuine affinity. If such was the case, Kamal was killed for it.

Either could be true. Or both. Kamal was human, after all.

Abuse is abuse, but the far more common offense is neglect. Just as far more people neglect their children than hit them, the most ordinary form of human unkindness to strangers is that we pass them by on the other side. Or send them away in the Happy Bus. Horton was there the day that the Happy Bus brought a group of mentally ill detainees up from Bucca. When interviewed, the detainees claimed that they had been inveigled onto the bus by the promise that it was bringing them home. To put it mildly, they were not happy to find themselves pulling up to the gates of Abu Ghraib instead.

Any American prison must admit to a percentage (3–15 percent) of mentally ill prisoners, but Abu Ghraib boasted more than its share, for obvious reasons. If Iraq had once had a National Institute of Mental Health, it didn't anymore, and the troublesome schizophrenic, clinically depressed, or dipsomaniacal joined the failed suicide bomber Thumby, and who knows how many innocents, behind the wire; there was nowhere else to go.

A detainee, mentally ill or otherwise, who in his pre–Abu Ghraib life had been an insurgent, a terrorist, or just a criminal, did not tend to show much improvement after spending a few months in the enclosures of Ganci, let alone any signs of rehabilitation.

On the other hand, a detainee who had been an ordinary citizen back in Anbar Province before being caught in the wrong place at the wrong time had every opportunity to make a move in the direction of insurgency, terrorism, criminality, or craziness.

So the guy who would catch an American's eye and slowly draw an index finger across his own throat, thus demonstrating the all-too-imaginable fate that awaited captive Americans, might have been serious and genuine in his threats. He could also have just been crazy. Each situation required different and delicate handling, and the Mainers had little to no way to differentiate the two.

One especially incensed detainee on the bus from Bucca was not only pitching a fit, he was threatening to hurl the contents of his colostomy bag, which was, in any case, overdue for refreshment.

"You can just go ahead and change it out," one of the escort soldiers said to Horton.

"We need a medic for that," Horton pointed out.

"C'mon. You can do it. Mostly, you just need enough guys to pin this asshole down," the delivering MP said cheerfully.

"No," said Horton firmly. "I am not going to do that. My guys do not have the skills to change a colostomy bag even on a cooperative detainee; I am not going to put this guy on the ground for an amateur procedure. You need to take him over to the CASH and get it done right."

The MP said something along the lines of *cheeeeeezum*, but he did as Horton asked.

"That poor guy . . . all those guys . . . they were *defenseless*," Horton would later say to Dizl and the others. "You know? *Defenseless*."

"I'm able to report that all of my soldiers are healthy and well," the *Portland Press Herald* quoted Captain Trevino in an article as the countdown to going home began.

Morale, he continued, remained good, in part because soldiers were able to communicate with their families via satellite phones and webcams attached to the computers in the command post.

It was a brand-new command post, built under the direction of some of the versatile field artillery/MP soldiers from the 152nd. "We can build it and we can blow it up!" Staff Sergeant Vigue quipped about the post to Major General Miller during one of the general's tours of inspection.

Naturally, as New Englanders, the Mainers cheered when the Boston Red Sox and the New England Patriots won their respective championships. Access to news seemed a more mixed blessing when, just before Christmas, they learned that two fellow Mainers—Sergeant Thomas Dostie of Somerville and Staff Sergeant Lynn Poulin Sr. of Freedom—were among the twenty-two Americans who died when a member of the Iraqi insurgent group Ansar al-Sunna snuck into a mess tent at a US base near Mosul and blew himself up.

Huladog never went home on leave during the whole yearlong deployment at Abu Ghraib. His was a calm and constant presence.

At Christmastime, a package of drawings from Maine children arrived, among them a second-grader's drawing of an American flag. Dizl hung it beside the door of the Mortar Café. The red-and-white stripes were carefully rendered, and a single star stood as a minimalist representation of the fifty states.

"Dear Mr. Thorndike," the artist wrote beneath the flag in careful, crayoned letters. "Thank you for your service. Please don't die."

As the soldiers left for their watches at Ganci, this became an acceptable, affectionate farewell.

"Don't die!"

"Roger that."

Out of the misery and horror of war, a strange blessing emerges in the form of the enduring, fierce love a warrior feels for those who have served in and endured combat with him. Though it's difficult to say if this blessing is worth the cost.

Nothing builds camaraderie like mutual suffering, and suffer the men did. Days and nights, when not filled with explosive shells, were filled with dread and intense boredom. This was dread based on real intel and an honest assessment of the sheer tactical and numerical disadvantage. And yet, in those moments, Dizl could turn to Huladog or Sugar, Parker or Hutton, a man or a woman, younger or older, skin color a non-factor because blood is red and would quite possibly paint everything and everyone soon enough, and Dizl could say, "I'm scared."

Whoever it was would answer, "Yeah. Me too."

Then Dizl could head off to do his work with the complete assurance that his comrades would prevent his head from being sawn off, or his burnt limbless body from ending up hung from those prison walls; they would prevent his death from being a show on the Internet for the world and his family to see. His comrades would thwart it, or die trying. He knew, and was glad to know that each of them held an identical, fully justified conviction that Dizl would do the same for them.

They risked death just to get him home for a funeral; it stood to reason they would unhesitatingly volunteer their life as sacrament to save another. Hell, history is full of soldiers and Marines, the unspoken heroes, who've lost their lives simply trying to recover the body of one of their comrades. There are things worse than death—failing the brother, or sister, on your left or on your right, for example. War takes so much, but at least you have your guys.

Long after Ganci made way for Redemption and the beginning of what seemed like a whole new epoch at Abu Ghraib, veteran Iraqi detainees would introduce Dizl to the newcomers as Shahein.

"This is Shahein," they would say, in Arabic, and the new man's eyes would grow wide.

"*Marhabah, ismey Shahein,*" Dizl would affirm. "Hello, I am Shahein."

While he was away in Maine, attending his Gram's funeral, longtime detainees at Abu Ghraib began asking where Shahein had gone.

"His grandmother died," Captain Trevino told them. "He went home to America for the funeral."

On his first day back on the job, Dizl was letting twenty or so detainees out of their enclosure for lunch and he cut his finger on the wire door. It started bleeding quite severely.

A detainee named Mastfa, a very religious man in his late thirties, said something in Arabic. All the detainees sat down on the ground inside the wire.

"What are you doing?"

"We will eat when your hand is taken care of," said Mastfa. "Not before."

In Arabic, he said—and the others repeated—"Shahein is a good man."

So here, too, was an unexpected gift of war, a bewildering one offered to Dizl in the House of Strange Fathers.

Getting to his feet, Mastfa hugged Dizl. "I will pray for your grandmother, Shahein," he said.

Sometime later, Mastfa was informed that his mother had died of a heart attack. Mastfa began to wail, and the detainees in his tent tried to console him. Some MPs—not guys from Maine, Dizl was glad to note—were annoyed by the wailing and they wanted to pull the mourner out to segregate him.

Dizl stood protectively in the doorway of Mastfa's tent. He waited there, his body screening and defending Mastfa's sanctuary, until the other MPs went away.

Some were muttering "hajji lover" under their breaths. Dizl took no real offence; the lover must love.

Redemption was a whole lot better than the disastrous Ganci, but if the camp was going to live up to its name, it would only come moment by moment, brick by brick, action by action over a long period of time. It would be up to the Mainers.

At one point, there was a small, handicapped Iraqi boy who lived in the place called the House of Ravens and Strange Fathers. One day, the dry blue sky began to rain explosives, and everyone ran for cover.

The detainees were diving into their new bomb shelters to hunker down behind their stacks of sandbags, but the little boy stood in the open. Perhaps he didn't know what was happening, or wasn't sure what to do. He was mentally handicapped in some way, and he was young. When children must face the instinctive choice of fight or flee, they tend to yield to a third option: freeze.

So the child froze. He stood there, stock still, in the lane between two long walls of wire, not far from the isolation cage where Shriek and Red had waited out a previous attack, as the rockets *wwheeerrr-rrrr*'d past on their various destructive paths.

Then three people, strangers who had flown a thousand miles across an unimaginable ocean as if for this sole purpose, flung their bodies over the child. Dizl, Shirley, and Sugar shielded his small body with theirs.

The Iraqi insurgency used civilians as shields; Dizl, Shirley, and Sugar became the shields. That is the difference between Good Guys and Bad.

EIGHTEEN

TROOP GREETERS

"The character of our military through history, the daring of Normandy, the fierce courage of Iwo Jima, the decency and idealism that turned enemies into allies is fully present in this generation. When Iraqi civilians looked into the faces of our service men and women, they saw strength and kindness and good will."

—President George W. Bush, May 1, 2003

To this day, Dizl doesn't sleep well because mortars fall into his dreams. The dream mortars are just as loud as the real ones were. Try sleeping through a 120 mm mortar that has landed on your roof. Thunder wakes him up in the night.

"Thunder," his significant other has learned to mumble, sleepy but reassuring.

Ah, right. Thunder. Normal stuff.

Traumatic stress is an obvious feature of combat and can result in what used to be called "soldier's heart," "shell shock," or "battle fatigue." We now know it as post-traumatic stress disorder, which has passed into ordinary discourse in the form of the acronym PTSD.

Occasionally one comes across estimates of the prevalence of PTSD among returning veterans that are as high as 40 percent. Chaplain Andy Gibson disputes this vigorously.

"PTSD is a diagnosis that becomes more common when the treatment is covered by insurance," he says. "Insurance companies often pay not by the hour, but by the diagnosis. There are strong incentives for mental health providers to write something definitive on the forms, and even if they explain to their patients that this is merely preliminary, any mental health diagnosis tends to be self-fulfilling.

"Anyone who has been in combat conditions for any length of time—certainly a year is plenty—will develop behaviors that are adaptive, that are *healthy, within that environment*. And anyone transitioning from that environment to a normal, peacetime environment is going to need considerable time to readjust his or her responses. Furthermore, that readjustment is going to be unpleasant. It's going to hurt.

"What the returning soldier needs, more than anything," Gibson emphasizes, "is *time*."

Ours is a nation in which the military is controlled—thankfully—by an elected civilian government. Yet we are encouraged in the widespread and dangerous illusion that the violence and bloodshed of America's wars have nothing to do with our ordinary lives. Thus, even if the war in Iraq, or any war, represents the spiritual and moral problem of human violence, it isn't really *our* problem. *We fight them over there so we don't have to fight them here.*

Those who like vicarious thrills can watch Brad Pitt or Kiefer Sutherland injure and kill people in dramatic and stylized slow motion, and those who like to think of themselves as followers of Christ or Muhammad or Buddha can find ways to justify or deplore violence without ever having to consider the ways in which they are served by it.

Relatively "few" of the hundreds of thousands of American troops who served in Iraq and Afghanistan lost their lives as a result. A "mere" 1–4 percent, depending on how you count it, actually died in combat or of combat-related injuries. The number climbs when you account for veteran suicide. This cannot be directly attributed to a combat deployment, though PTSD significantly raises the risk of suicide in an individual.

What people hear is that more troops survived wounds, and they regard "not dead" as a synonym for "returned home safe." More than thirty-five thousand Purple Heart medals have been given to those injured during the war in Iraq. No one can return to a life of normalcy after such experiences as being shot or blown up.

Injured or not, many, and perhaps most, of the troops who served in combat in this generation's wars, as in past wars, came home changed into someone else. If you talk to combat veterans or to their loved ones, positive changes may be noted.

"He grew up over there," fathers of young combat veterans might say. "He takes life seriously now." Still, a father must wince when he says this, as if his son's maturity, however welcome, is a benefit that came at a cost too high to calculate.

"I am not who I was," Dizl and Turtle declared to one another, and they couldn't even have said whether the change was for better or worse, only that it had happened, was huge, and would prove permanent.

Deliberate, organized violence has a long pedigree as a maturational rite of passage from boy to man, but presumably President George W. Bush did not attack Iraq so children of this generation would have an opportunity to grow up, any more than the Vietnam-era draft was in place so that the boys of Bush's generation would have an opportunity to become men.

The varied effects of combat on the people who have served, been wounded or maimed, been changed, or who died in the midst of a war are immaterial. They are no more the point of the exercise than the death of Saddam's infant daughter from an American bomb, the destruction of a baby food factory, or the looting of Iraqi national treasures. The point of a war is to accomplish by force some aim that cannot be accomplished in any other way. If a nation is, or at least aspires to be, a moral nation, then the aim must be legitimate, and important enough to justify the material and moral cost. We must acknowledge and pay the high costs of war.

"Don't die," the small boy wrote, and none of them did. The men of the 152nd came home, all of them, with hearts, brains, guts, spines, and balls all still more or less connected. Some had come very close to death, a mere turn of the head or the shifting of weight from one foot to the other being the difference between living and dying.

Many had friends from other units who had not been so lucky.

Chiclets couldn't save the life of his friend, a Marine who had been too close when an IED exploded outside the prison gates. The combat medic held his friend's head together with his hands, trying to keep his dear and necessary brain from falling out, and watched as the life left his friend's face. He has to live with that.

This gentle young man was, however, able to save the life of the Iraqi who had detonated the improvised explosive device, then been subsequently injured and captured by retaliating US soldiers. That man killed Chiclets's friend. He has to live with that, too. In this one act, in saving the life of the man who killed his friend, Chiclets showed a love of humanity that would humble Christ himself. He, too, was a *hajji lover*, and there is now one fewer Iraqi family with a justified hatred of America.

When the 306th MP Brigade arrived in January 2005 to take over the Sixteenth MPs' duties, Abu Ghraib could still, without a doubt, be described as dirty and dangerous. The insurgency was still going strong, and the prison was still smack in the middle of it, geographically and symbolically. The facility retained most of its strategic disadvantages—no one had moved the highways, for example—so mortar, rocket, and sniper attacks remained a common feature of daily life.

But the prisoners were now housed in the clean, well-organized, and relatively secure Camp Redemption, sorted among the holding areas with their air-conditioned tents by age, health, and the level of risk presented.

The troops, meanwhile, now had a gym, a BX/PX (a shop where personal items might be purchased), a KBR laundry unit, volleyball and basketball courts, and an Internet center.

Abu Ghraib now was home to the 115th Combat Support Hospital with doctors, nurses, operating theaters, and an intensive-care unit where, among others, Ahmad al-Shayea, the suicide bomber, was treated after he survived the December 2004 detonation of the VBIED he was driving. "I came to help the Iraqis," he told American researcher Ken Ballen. "But when I needed help . . . the Americans were the ones who helped me."[12]

Rumsfeld was right back in May of 2004. The detainee abuse photographed by Graner, England, and company did not represent America. It did not represent American values and it certainly did not represent the values of Colonel Quantock's Sixteenth MP Brigade at Abu Ghraib. However, this is not true merely because the secretary of defense declared it to be. It was, instead, a truth lived out by the men from Maine and their comrades from Ohio, Pennsylvania, and Puerto Rico, the Americans inaugurating the long work of redemption through the blood, the shit (actual and metaphorical), the ambiguity, and the excruciating physical, psychological, and spiritual pain of Abu Ghraib.

Who are you? asked the eyes of the detainees, who watched as Shirley, Sugar, and Dizl shielded the child's body with their own.

---

12 Ballen, *Terrorists in Love,* 40.

We are Americans. This is how we roll.

Concussive injuries of all kinds are cumulative. Dizl's original traumatic brain injury was exacerbated by repeated exposure to explosions in Iraq. To this day, he has problems with memory, with mood, and with maintaining the coherence of his thoughts. These are normal manifestations of the underlying injury, yet when Dizl first went to the VA hospital to have his war wounds treated, he was asked whether he could provide proof that his injuries were, in fact, sustained in Iraq.

"Do you have any witnesses?" the screener asked.

"Well, there's the lieutenant," Dizl replied. "But he's still deployed. And Parker was there, but . . . he's . . ."

The claims officer looked at him expectantly.

"Well, he died," said Dizl. "Parker died. Not then, I mean. Later."

"Well, sir, you'll need to get *some* sort of documentation to support your petition. A statement from your living witness would be helpful."

The idea of trying to navigate the VA bureaucracy with an injured brain and a heart sick with grief is appalling enough to make suicide among war vets seem explicable.

The indignity of having to prove your own wartime injuries was only exacerbated when Dizl talked to civilians about his deployment.

"Oh, you were in Iraq?" they ask to this day. "Where did you serve?"

"Abu Ghraib."

"Really. How many Iraqis did you torture?"

Since the 152nd's return, Abu Ghraib—the prison, not the town—has been closed, but the pain of Abu Ghraib continues, and will continue until it finds itself and loses itself in love. This is what happens with wars, especially those that are ambiguous even beyond the essential ambiguity of any war.

Some of Dizl's pain is expressed as outrage, as the anger that is the voice of love, frustrated: *How could you, Donald Rumsfeld? How could you, Lynndie England? How could you, insurgent on the overpass? Why wasn't Kamal, or Shriek, or Young Elvis—even just that one, smiling, innocent boy—worth enough to stay your hand?*

Before the Americans arrived at the Abu Ghraib prison, many thousands drew their last, tormented breaths there. Their bodies were discarded and turned to bones in the sand, bones for Dizl to later collect and attempt to reassemble.

Then other Iraqis died, right in front of him, blown to pieces by insurgent bombs, and he and his comrades helped gather up the pieces of men and boys whose names they had known. Now Dizl sits on the shore beside a cold sea, watching the water wash the stones.

In the end, all the enormous expenditure of human effort, along with three hundred million dollars, at last proved insufficient to overcome the strangeness of the House of Strange Fathers and Redemption. With America and her prisoners of war as its last tenant, the whole facility—Hard Site, Mortar Café, DFAC, CASH, torture cells, Redemption—all of it was razed.

As of December 18, 2011, the American war in Iraq is over. The last American convoys crossed the border into Kuwait, armored-up and under conditions of such secrecy that the soldiers were not able to say good-bye to the Iraqis who had served with them.

Interviewed on NPR, Michael White, of icasualties.org, said that the official American toll is 4,484 dead, with an estimated 32,000 wounded. The cost to the American taxpayer begins with what was actually authorized for the wars in Afghanistan and Iraq together: $824 billion, but this does not include interest, because much of this money was borrowed, nor the long-term care of veterans. Continuing treatment for the men and women injured in these overlapping wars (many Americans are now veterans of both) is expected to cost between $600 billion and $1 trillion.

Asked to state the number of Iraqi civilians who lost their lives in the war, White refused to give a precise answer, but "it's in the hundreds of thousands." Most of these, of course, died not from American bombs or bullets, but at the hands of their fellow Iraqis. Still, absent the invasion, the majority of those who were killed would probably still be alive today. The guys from the 152nd could name a few.

"In absolute terms," wrote historian William R. Polk, "virtually every Iraqi has a parent, child, spouse, cousin, friend, colleague, or neighbor—or perhaps all of these—among the dead. More than half the dead were women and children." The long-term effects of warfare itself, regardless of the cause for which people are fighting, are, Polk reminds us, inevitably brutalizing.

"War should only take place as a final (unavoidable) option; when it does the wounds run deep and scars remain," said Captain—now Major—Philip Trevino.

If, six, seven, or eight years after returning from Iraq, a middle-aged man from Maine still studies the shoulder of I-95 as he drives, alert for IEDs; if he has to check the perimeter of a restaurant before he can bring himself to walk inside; if he can be startled into full-alert by a suddenly slamming door, or be beset by waves of rage or grief, then we can only assume there is a country full of men, women, and children on the other side of the world enduring this, too, and more.

While it is too soon to know, it is certainly possible that history will judge the American adventure in Iraq as a mistake. Within the existential confines of this war, there were certainly Americans who behaved dishonorably. However, many would, under conditions marked by physical danger and moral ambiguity, nonetheless manage to exemplify what is best in the American character: inventiveness, optimism, tenacity, a desire to defend the weak and champion the vulnerable, and an openhearted willingness to see a shared humanity in a designated enemy.

The Lost Boys, out of a job and packing up, had the remaining task of "transitioning-in" the soldiers of the 361st who had arrived to relieve them. The Mainers took this seriously, as memories of the brief, dispirited, and unhelpful orientation they had received from their own predecessors were still unpleasantly fresh in their minds.

"How much stick time do you get?" one new MP asked Dizl, slapping an imaginary nightstick against his open palm.

"Stick time?" Dizl repeated, dumbfounded. Then he was enraged. "*Stick time?*"

He had to swallow a sudden sense of despair: *Oh no. Oh shit. They're going to screw it up.* They would certainly be tested, just as the 152nd had been tested. The Bad Guys were gearing up for this already. Within weeks, in fact, Al-Qaeda in Iraq would launch another major mass casualty attack on Abu Ghraib designed to take advantage of the inexperience of the new team. It would be recorded as the largest single assault on an American forward base since the Vietnam War. Thanks to Redemption's bomb shelters and all those sandbags, at least no detainee would die that day.

One thousand one . . . here it was, the last mortar attack of the 152nd's deployment, a kiss-off from al-Zarqawi.

Some of the new guys were in the next room when the explosions began. The Lost Boys had hit the deck by en masse instinct, and were now squashed companionably together on the floor.

A 120 mm rocket landed on the roof, and though it did not explode—they would all have been dead—the impact was jarring, and the Lost Boys could hear the new guys screaming. They offered the traditional military comfort: *Welcome to Abu Ghraib, you bastards. Now suck it up, get going. And do it the way it should be done, you hear? This is your war, now.*

On their last day, it rained. Everything—the sand, the sky, the soldiers' skins, their boots and uniforms, the helicopters and the

helo pad they crossed to reach the cafeteria where one more pow-
dered-egg breakfast awaited them—was brownish gray, dulled by
rain and mud made of the ever-present dirt and the long-decayed
remains of an untold number of human beings.

Dizl walked behind the younger members of the platoon, his feet
matching theirs in the automatic rhythm of a march. An artist first
and last, Dizl was meditating on the color of the Iraqi desert after
a rain has fallen and the strange fact that he, a forty-year-old army
reserve private from the coast of Maine, had come to know so inti-
mately the colors and contours of so alien a place.

Even the puddles on the tarmac were that brownish gray, reflect-
ing the barest sheen of tarnished silver light. Gathered around the
edges of these were hundreds, no, *thousands* of tiny, thirsty moths,
their wings camouflaged in the color of the omnipresent dust, sip-
ping the short-lived moisture while they could.

Having spied these, Shahein opened his mouth to call out, "Hey
boys, check out the moths." Looking up, he stopped, transfixed. The
boys, his boys, were walking toward their ride home, oblivious. Each
time a booted foot landed in a puddle, the moths around its edge
flew upward, like a slow-motion splash, and the undersides of their
wings were a beautiful, shimmering blue. It was as if their footprints
bloomed the blue of forget-me-nots, or as if these soldiers, all-un-
knowing, released with every step a thousand fragments of a Maine
summer sky.

Transport had been arranged and then—FRAGO—rearranged, as
helicopters became available, then unavailable, then available again.
The men of the 152nd had packed most of the big stuff into the conex
boxes, so they could clamber into the open trucks for the ride out to
BIAP with only what Turtle referred to as their "carry-on luggage."

"Hey, Dizl," Lunch Lady called from his truck. "Hop up here. I
can hold your guitar so it won't get wet."

Beerboy's mother had already sent an email, liberally laced with joyous exclamation marks, to relatives, friends, and neighbors letting everyone know that, within mere days, her son and his comrades would be back home in Maine. Prayers of thanksgiving would rise from the steeples of Lincolnville's old country church. The men of the 152nd would be greeted at Bangor Airport by troop greeters offering chocolate chip cookies, and at the National Guard armory by their families holding bunches of bright flowers. Chaplain Andrew Gibson, whose eyes had filled with tears when they departed, would feel his eyes fill again when the roll was called and every name had a voice to answer with.

When the Mainers returned to the United States, they were asked to fill out self-assessment questionnaires intended to reveal the actual or potential mental health effects of their service at Abu Ghraib.

Q. Did you see any American Service Members killed in action?

Huladog points out that they didn't ask whether the soldier saw any Iraqis die. Space was not given on the page to describe the day that the truck with the spotter appeared on the overpass, the day that forty-one detainees under the care and control of Maine's citizen-soldiers would be blown to pieces before their eyes, the screams of the dying mingling with urgent cries from the wounded.

No one on the committee that doubtless created the self-assessment questionnaire thought to ask whether, in view of the Islamic desire to bury all parts of a body before sunset, the Iraqi men had used their Styrofoam lunch plates to scoop up entrails, handing them through the concertina to the American men on the other side.

No one apparently considered the possibility that, when a desperate detainee (unshot, because the guard in the tower recognized in time that the head under his arm wasn't a bomb) tossed the severed head of his brother across the wire, the soldier on the other side would find that the head had been threaded onto his outstretched arm like a bead on a string.

Q. *Did you lose any personal friends while in Iraq?*

Did you feel a kinship with anyone who was not your friend, or a connection deeper than acquaintance, with the detainee who read your mind, interpreted your gestures, and allowed you to help him save his friends' lives?

Do you wish the Geneva Conventions weren't quite so particular about photographing detained persons, so that you could have a picture of Young Elvis munching crackers, instead of that memory of his small brown hand, waving at you as he ran by the tower, or the boy's voice as he called, "You are a good man, Shahein!" Even as your eyes fixed themselves on the man with binoculars on the overpass and time began its sickening crawl?

"You are a good man, Shahein."

This is what Dizl has to go by.

In his more somber moments, he fears most of the Iraqis he knew at Abu Ghraib are now dead: the ones whose mother-given names he knew, the ones he and his comrades named for themselves even as they were named in return, and the ones known to him only by their ID numbers.

He hopes the kids are OK, at least. Tat-twah and Bulbul, all the Little Rascals and Shriek too. Dizl hangs on to the hope that they are well, happy, and doing good things with their lives, and that whether Kamal was a saint—as Yogi believes—or a sinner, Kamal's daughter should by now be prom queen and president of her graduating class. One can hope, anyway.

War movies almost always seem to end with the triumphant return of the troops. As if victory, or making it home safe, is the only thing a warrior needs to return to his old self. Even after the credits and the welcome home parties drift into fond memory, the movie still plays for Dizl, whether he wants it to or not. It is indeed his very humanism that keeps his dreams haunted.

Dizl has tears in his eyes when he says he's named some of his egg-laying hens after Iraqi detainees. "Because I miss them."

The American people sit there, themselves teetering on the edge of a well full of poverty, depression, or any of the other monsters loosed from Pandora's Box, laughing at—or dismissing—the others around them falling in. They don't realize there are those around and among them being pulled into that well by weights they hung around their own necks on the behalf of the American people.

Every second Dizl is home is the first second of the rest of his life as he bears his moral weight. The moment-by-moment struggle to stay loving despite the burden of mental injury and the horrific memories. The fight for survival started when the first mortar exploded, showering Dizl with dirt and debris from a country not his own, and has not ended. Perhaps it never will.

One thousand one . . .

ACKNOWLEDGMENTS

FIRST AND FOREMOST, I'd like to thank Dizl, Hula, and all the men of the 152nd. Words will never be able to capture the entirety of your heroism and service to this country. It is an honor to play my part in sharing this piece of your story. You showed the world who the best of America—and Maine—are. You make me proud to call this great state home. I'd also like to thank my mother. This project reminded me a lot of the homeschool years, the collaboration on papers and short stories that set the mold for the writer I am today. Thank you for that gift and so many others. I love you. I'd also like to tip my hat to my editor, Maxim, for being so patient with me and to Shaun, my agent, for his efforts in finding the right publisher.